Watch Me Grow:
I'm One

"I love this book! As a trainer working with parents and professionals, I've been waiting for a book like this. It is a gem. Its storytelling style brings us into the mind of the one-year-old and helps answer the age-old questions that we have about infants: What are they thinking? And why are they doing that? Maureen has given a voice to one-year-olds that we can all understand and gives us a window into their world. It is a mixture of the most current research, information on development and age appropriate behavior, the sound advice of an expert, and the empathy of a friend. I will be using this book as a resource in all the classes that I teach and recommend it to others. I'm already looking forward to *Watch Me Grow: I'm Two* and the rest of the series. I hope Maureen is a fast writer!"

—MARLIES ZAMMUTO, deputy executive director of Education and Program Development, Child Care Circuit

WATCH ME GROW:

I'm One

EVERY PARENT'S GUIDE TO THE ENCHANTING 12- TO 24-MONTH-OLD

BY **MAUREEN O'BRIEN, Ph.D.,**
WITH **SHERILL TIPPINS**

WILLIAM MORROW
An Imprint of HarperCollinsPublishers

A Skylight Press Book

HarperCollins books may be purchased for educational, business, or sales promotional use. For information please write: Special Markets Department, HarperCollins Publishers Inc., 10 East 53rd Street, New York, NY 10022.

FIRST EDITION

Photographs by Elise Sinagra Donoghue
Book design by Gretchen Achilles
Printed on acid-free paper
Library of Congress CIP Data has been applied for.
ISBN 0-688-16878-7
00 01 02 03 04 QW 10 9 8 7 6 5 4 3 2 1

To

My four guys

Dad, George, Alexander, and Matthew

and

to

Vincent and Dash

ACKNOWLEDGMENTS

Both formal and informal "teachers" have helped me understand children and parenting and therefore have made my writing this book possible. The diverse families I have met through my work at Children's Hospital in Boston, Temple University, and the Institute of Child Development at the University of Minnesota taught me so much about the essence of parenting. My mentors at these institutions deserve special thanks, as they showed me how to turn my innate fascination with children into observational skills and to see families' behavior as theory in action. In particular, T. Berry Brazelton and my colleagues at the Touchpoints Project have deeply influenced my perspective of families—as the experts they are. My own family of origin and the wonderful family I am now blessed to be raising have helped shape me immeasurably, of course. So, thanks, Mom and Dad, Jim, Tom, and Trish, as well as the Garcia clan for all your support and for your example.

MAUREEN O'BRIEN

CONTENTS

Watch Me Grow:
I'm One

INTRODUCTION

The two women sat talking on a park bench in the playground, so near that I couldn't help but overhear. They were discussing a parent support group that they had been trying to organize but were frustrated because they'd had difficulty getting experts to come speak to them.

"It's not fair," one of them said, only half joking as she gently pushed her baby's stroller back and forth. "My sister's receptionist has a really bad home situation, and she has all kinds of social services helping her out with the kids. She gets counseling, parenting classes, lists of baby-care services. It makes me feel guilty to say it, but I need help sometimes, too, and there's nobody there for me. I don't have to worry about child abuse or physical handicaps with my baby, but I still need *help!*"

As the mother of twin five-year-old boys, I could sympathize with her frustration. She was doing her best to adjust to her new situation as a mother, trying to raise her child in a responsible way and enjoy doing it at the same time. But sometimes one feels so isolated as a new parent— trying to get by on instinct, contradictory advice from friends, and generic advice from child-care books that often seem dated—that it seems impossible to do a good enough job. As a developmental psychologist and former director of the Touchpoints Project, a nationally known child-development program at Boston Children's Hospital, I'm well aware of the constantly growing bank of research on how babies and young children learn and grow. I appreciate how this information can help parents help their children reach their full potential while enjoying a richer, smoother family life. The trouble is, I also know how often this priceless information—from the most recent findings on brain development to a compendium of parent-tested methods of solving everyday problems—fails to find its way to the parents who need it most.

Years of experience working with a wide variety of parent support groups, from "at risk" parents struggling against poverty to middle-class couples stressed out by the demands of child plus job, have taught me much about universal parent concerns. The crucial advantage any parent, regardless of background, can have is the knowledge that he or she has a supportive, informed person to turn to—whether that person is a child-development expert, a pediatrician, a relative, or a competent friend. When we feel overwhelmed by a situation, failing to understand why our child is behaving a certain way, a well-informed support person can help us step back from the conflict. Ideally, he or she can help us to understand how the child feels and what he is trying to communicate, and to consider which of a number of solutions might both alleviate the problem and reinforce the relationship between parent and child. Again and again, I have observed how just knowing that that friend was there for them, ready to lend a hand when necessary, has helped parents recover their equilibrium and improve their family life.

When I became a parent, I came across the challenges we all experience—conflicts with my little ones that I hadn't anticipated when pregnant, even situations I'd never run into in my work. Like most parents, I turned to books at times when I needed backup, for either information or reassurance. The classics were helpful—particularly Dr. Spock's *Baby and Child Care* with its reminder that parents know more than they think they do. My day-to-day interactions at work with Dr. T. Berry Brazelton brought to life the importance of considering the unique aspects of each parent-child combination. What I felt was missing from many of the sources I'd found, though, was a voice to which I could personally relate—the voice of another mother who had the background of a career in child development and who had recently been through these early years of parenting and could apply her knowledge to real-life, practical situations.

My parenting experience deepened my formal training in a way that only hands-on trial and error can. My twins taught me how important it is to respect the individual nature of each child and why a one-size-fits-all approach to parenting is doomed to fall short in a world in which every child develops at his own rate. I also saw, over and over, how knowledge unearthed through recent research on brain development could be used in everyday situations to help babies and young children build healthier, happier lives. Most important, I understood from personal experience that both children and parents are growing, changing beings who learn from *each other,* and that both child development and parenting are processes that evolve over time.

Now, with this book, and all the books in the *Watch Me Grow* series, I hope to offer you the fruits of my training and experience—to act as *your* supportive, well-informed resource, helping you to understand exactly "what's going in that little head" on those days when you feel at odds with your child. It is my firm conviction that you don't need a Ph.D. to be the best parent you can be. All you need to do is observe your little one, get to know her individual style, and take advantage of the wonderful array of scientific and practical information provided here. Together we will explore all the amazing accomplishments and challenges your baby is likely to experience between twelve and twenty-four months—acknowledging how each new change in behavior can affect the entire family while also looking at the transformation from the *child's* point of view. By alternating sensible approaches to common concerns such as sleep disruption and speech delays with clear, useful explanations of how your child's body is learning to work in conjunction with her brain, I can share with you all the knowledge and confidence that my formal training has given me. Anecdotes collected from other parents may provide you with new insights and remind you that you're not the only person to have traveled this road. "Q&A" sections address some of the more challenging dilemmas that arise when parenting a one-year-old. Descriptions of toddlers at work at the toy box will show you how young children learn and grow. Finally, a "First-Person Singular" section at the end of each chapter allows you to write down your observations of your own child's behavior—comparing it to the descriptions you've found here, contrasting it with earlier behavior, and noting any questions it brings to mind. Here you can record what kinds of activities your child likes best, how her energy level tends to fluctuate throughout the day, how she responds to your various parenting "experiments," and what the warning signs are that she's used up her energy and needs a break. This accumulated knowledge will help you adjust your parenting style to her ever-evolving needs.

Every child is a unique being, with his or her own personality and way of growing. The best use of this and other books is as a departure point for your own research into why your child acts as he or she does and which parenting techniques work best. The new knowledge and fresh insight offered here will give you much of the information you need to parent your one-year-old successfully. Direct observation will do the rest. It is my hope that by showing you new ways to look at, listen to, and respond to your little one, this book will lift some of the weight of parenthood from your shoulders, empowering you to do what you naturally want to do—share the joy of living with your delightful one-year-old and introduce your child to all the wonders of the world.

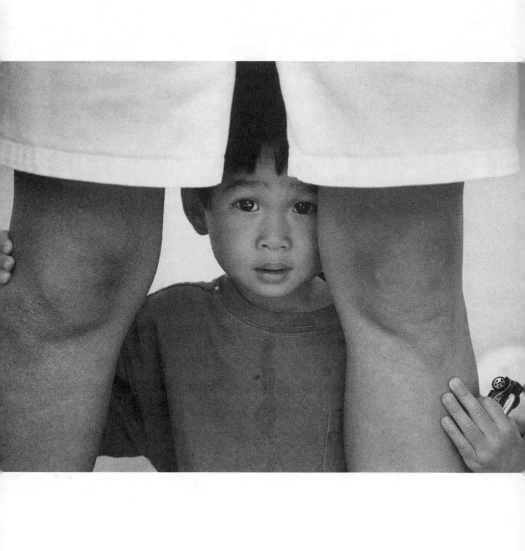

What I'm Like

At birth your baby's brain is one-fourth its adult size. By his second birthday, it will be three-quarters its adult size.

What a pleasure it is to see a child move from the nearly total dependence of his first twelve months toward a life filled with exploration, verbal communication, and active learning. Mom and Dad watch proudly as fifteen-month-old Philip sits on the floor of their living room, babbling happily as he plays with the plastic rings and spindle they gave him for his birthday. Over the past three months, he has learned to bang the rings against the spindle, pull himself to his feet so he can throw a ring to the floor, and then, when Dad picks up one of the rings, stagger over to try to take it from him. Now, as he puts the first ring on the spindle, then the next, Philip's smile grows in amazement—and so do his parents'. He dares to reach for a third. Uh-oh. This one doesn't fit. Philip furrows his brow. He pushes, hard. It won't budge. Suddenly, to his parents' dismay, Philip lets out a yell and sends the toy flying across the room. *It won't let me put the ring on!* he's thinking. *Bad toy! I hate it!*

Such is the dilemma of the one-year-old—determined enough to know what he wants, but increasingly aware that he's not quite able to get it. No wonder the generally eager, sunny disposition of the twelve- to fifteen-month-old begins to succumb to bouts of angry tears, yelling, and "acting out" more and more as he approaches midyear. Who wouldn't want to cry if his feet slipped out from under him every time he tried to run? Who wouldn't protest loudly if Mom disappeared for work with no clear indication of when she'd return? And who wouldn't kick and squirm if his caregiver pinned him down for a diaper change just when he wanted to chase the cat?

Being the parent of a one-year-old is all about reveling in those exciting periods when your child's physical and mental capabilities suddenly take a giant leap forward. It's also all about supporting him through the difficult periods—the times when he knows what skill he wants to master (walking, asking for his blanket, putting on his shoes) but hasn't quite done it yet. Certainly, there are plenty of rewards in store for you this year. During the next twelve months, your baby will begin to appreciate what's out there in the world for him: the colors of a flower, the pleasure of sipping apple juice on a hot day, and the joy of watching a bird fly. He'll discover the satisfactions of banging on the kitchen pans while you cook dinner, clutching a favorite blankie as he learns to lull himself to sleep, and eagerly climbing stairs, furniture, and even people. As he approaches age two, he will grow increasingly interested in others. He'll begin to learn how to converse with his caregiver, his grandfather, and the lady next door, and he'll learn to play happily alongside other children, even if he's not always directly interacting with them. His increasing social awareness will help him begin to sense other people's emotional states, learn to take turns (sometimes), and begin to control his negative impulses in ways that will encourage friendship.

Nevertheless, there will be times—probably around the middle of this year—when his whining, banging, or loud, repeated "No!" will baffle and discourage you. These negative behaviors are not a sign of naughtiness or rebellion; rather, they are natural expressions of frustration as your child learns to cope with a tidal wave of new feelings and developing (but not fully developed) capabilities. In fact, those times when your one-year-old seems to fall apart without any visible provocation are some of the surest indicators that he is developing at a healthy, normal pace. (It might also help keep things in perspective to know that, according to a 1986 study by T. Power and M. Chapieski, toddlers are *told* no every nine minutes on average.) By focusing on how to arrange and manage his environment so that he encounters as few no-win situations as possible—by erecting a supportive scaffolding of predictable rules, practices, and routines—you can help him realize his new goals in ways that won't overwhelm him, and that will help you maintain your own equilibrium as well. Fortunately, this is far from a thankless task. By supporting him in his growth, you'll have the pleasure of participating in his transformation from alert but profoundly dependent babyhood to the active, eager, increasingly independent state of early childhood. Best of all, by the time he turns two, your little one will be able to communicate his appreciation by telling you he loves you in his very own words.

Where's Grandma?

"Beh!" Twelve-month-old Jeffrey points to the teddy bear in his toy basket and looks expectantly at Grandma, who's baby-sitting tonight.

"Bear!" she responds with gratifying enthusiasm, picking up the bear and handing it to him. "Is this your favorite bear, Jeffrey? What's his name?"

Jeffrey doesn't understand the word "favorite" but is about to respond anyway, when abruptly the noise of a telephone cuts through the air. *Loud!*

Jeffrey claps his hands over his ears. The muffling effect intrigues him. Focusing on his hearing, he shifts his attention away from Grandma. Then the telephone stops ringing. Jeffrey looks up.

No Grandma. Jeffrey looks around, stunned. The room suddenly looks enormous. He feels chilled and frightened. *Alone!* Instinctively, he starts to crawl toward the doorway. At the door, he stands up and peeks into the hall. *Grandma's voice!* He can hear it! Too eager to try walking, he drops down again and crawls down the hall at top speed.

There she is, in the dining room, talking on the phone. *Grandma!* At the sight of her Jeffrey pauses, overcome with relief. He crawls over, grabs her skirt, and pulls himself to his feet. "Aaah!" he says, holding on to her knees.

"Hello, Jeffrey," she says, smiling, and puts a hand on his head as she turns back to the phone. Jeffrey basks in the pleasure of her touch. *Wanted Grandma*, he thinks with great satisfaction. *Got her!* He looks down at his feet and stamps the floor with satisfaction.

STAGGERING TOWARD INDEPENDENCE: YOUR CHILD'S PROGRESS IN THE SECOND YEAR

There is something about a one-year-old's taking his first unaided step that invites parents to sit back, take a deep breath, and congratulate themselves on how far their little one has come. This feeling of pride is well deserved. Your wide-eyed neophyte of a year ago has learned an amazing amount in his short lifetime. He has developed from a contented little bundle to a rolling, then reaching, then sitting, creeping, crawling, and perhaps even staggering dynamo. He has moved from responding instinctively to random stimuli toward anticipating certain actions, recognizing familiar objects and surroundings, and developing a rudimentary memory. He has learned to tell the difference between speech and other sounds, to play with "ba-ba-ba" and "da-da-da" sound combinations, to babble constantly in his own jargon, and even to say a word or two in real language. Most enjoyably, he has moved from communicating mostly through crying to seeking eye contact, smiling at loved ones, fussing to demonstrate his displeasure when they leave, and engaging in simple games and play with others. By his first birthday, real signs of his unique character have emerged, giving you some tantalizing hints of just what kind of child—and adult—he may turn out to be.

In fact, your twelve-month-old probably appears as supremely pleased with himself as you are with him. His pride in his new ability to communicate his desire for a cookie, to reach and control the television set, and to crawl after a ball if it rolls away gives him a typically cheerful disposition. The reality, though, is that beneath this placid self-sufficiency rumbles the drumbeat of major change. As we will see in Chapter 2, the body of that twelve-month-old playing happily on the floor has already begun gearing up for the enormous transformation into an upright, habitually walking state. The urge to practice walking will become practically irresistible between twelve and eighteen months—though his actual progress may be sporadic, involving "plateaus" in skill development that last several weeks or even longer. Whether or not he can yet get around on his own two feet, a child this age experiences great frustration at being confined and frequently expresses his feelings with tears and anger. As my colleague Dr. T. Berry Brazelton has pointed out in his book *Touchpoints,* the need to keep moving can even disrupt a one-year-old's sleep. Fortunately, these motor drives and their attendant side effects fade somewhat after about eighteen months in the face of a new focus on language and cognitive growth. After that, your little one may be better able to relax into a car seat, for example, if you talk with him or give him something interesting to play with.

Your one-year-old's increased ability to move around, explore, and experiment with objects will expose him to an enormous variety of fascinating new information. In Chapter 3, we will see how this interaction will teach him the concepts of empty and full, here and not-here, cause and effect. Predictable routines that you and others provide will help his brain develop the idea that events often take place in sequence—a discovery that will eventually help him understand the passage of time. As his memory improves, he will be able to learn more efficiently from daily experience. A better memory will also allow him to frame thoughts in his mind and hold on to them long enough to plan actions and carry them out deliberately.

Though he may already be able to say one, two, or even several recognizable words at the age of twelve months, your child's verbal abilities will really take off by around the middle of the second year, as his ability to frame thoughts improves. Though his verbal progress may be as sporadic as his motor development—and will only really progress when his ability to walk has been achieved—you can rest assured that even if he says nothing, he always understands much more than he can say. As we will learn in Chapter 4, your child could probably already respond to simple, two-word commands ("Come here") by his first birthday. By fifteen months, he will probably know, but not yet be able to say, the names of "his" people and pets. When children reach eighteen months, their spoken vocabulary often starts to increase at a rapid pace. "No" frequently becomes a favorite word. By the end of the second year, most will probably be able to speak in two-, three-, or four-word sentences (though the variance among children is very wide at this age) and understand perhaps two hundred words.

Much of your child's emotional development during this year wouldn't be possible without the physical, mental, and verbal progress that accompanies it. As we will see in Chapter 5, the twelve-month-old is just becoming aware that his thoughts are separate from those of others and are hidden from them unless he expresses them. This ability sharpens his interest in others' emotional states. Your child will begin to respond more to your emotional expressions. As the year progresses, his emotional energy will become increasingly focused on his desire to control his environment. Beginning at around fifteen to eighteen months, he will become easily frustrated when he cannot make things go the way he wants them to go. There may be howls of frustration as he decides *he* wants to be the one to leave when he feels like it; *he* wants to choose whether he wears shoes; *he* wants to decide whether he feels like eating. Since he is not yet able to reason or to consider long-term benefits, this can be a difficult time for you and your child. By the end of the year, though, his physical, mental, and verbal abilities will have caught up somewhat to his desire for independence, and he may become easier to get along with.

Your one-year-old's determination to walk, talk, think, and feel like a "big kid" will leave little room for socializing with other children during the first half of the year, but as his verbal, emotional, and mental growth continues, he will become increasingly able to turn outward and begin interacting with others. I will point out in Chapter 6 that the second half of the second year is an excellent time to begin arranging play dates, so your child can explore the idea of having a friend and so you can help him through the inevitable lessons in sharing, taking turns, and settling differences in acceptable ways.

All of this growth—physical, cognitive, verbal, emotional, and social—proceeds more comfortably for your child and your entire family if you are able to provide reliable routines for his daily life and enforce consistent limits that take his developmental stage into account. Chapters 7 and 8 are devoted to exploring ways in which to create predictable, but not rigid, routines for sleeping, eating, and other everyday activities and

Toddlers love to experiment with new textures, and self-feeding is a wonderful advance this year.

to begin teaching your child which behaviors are unacceptable to help him learn to govern himself.

Of course, there is no way to predict exactly when your child will achieve a particular milestone and no way to significantly hasten its arrival. "My friend Kathy and I had our first babies almost a month apart," a mother in a Washington, D.C., suburb recalled recently. "She and I grew up together, and the whole time we were pregnant, we talked about how much fun it would be to have kids who were best friends. The problem is that her son, Gabriel, always seems to accomplish things before mine does, even though he's three weeks younger than my Kevin. Gabe just had his first birthday, and when we're over at his house for a visit, he walks around like he owns the place, while Kevin sits in one spot and babbles. I just wonder sometimes what Kathy is doing that I'm not doing."

The answer, quite probably, is "Nothing." Despite our tendency to compare our kids to others, until a child is ready, there is not really much you can do to help him move forward except be patient and encourage the efforts he does make. Rest assured that he is not just sitting idle; he's working on other skills that you aren't focused on. Observe him carefully, looking for clues to what his current interests are so you can encourage them. Understand that his entire being is concentrated on learning to do precisely what you want him to do, but that the challenges of these very difficult and complex growth spurts will sometimes require him to rest, review old skills, and vent his frustration. And next time your best friend's one-year-old talks circles around your babbling little one, pick up your baby, give him a hug, and tell him he's the best conversationalist you've ever known.

EASING THE WAY
Planning Ahead

As your baby faces the enormous challenges of learning to walk, talk, and understand others' points of view, he is bound to run into frustrations practically every waking hour of his day. At times it is tempting just to impose circumstances on your toddler and let him wail (putting him in a playpen while you're on the telephone, for example, instead of letting him practice toddling around the living room), telling yourself that he needs to learn to deal with frustration in any case. Though it's true that learning to postpone gratification is a necessary skill, it's better learned at a later age. During this year, forcing your child frequently to endure a frustrating situation that makes him cry just wastes valuable time he could have spent developing his walking, communicating, or thinking abilities. Experienced parents and other caregivers will tell you that a more productive approach is to *think ahead,* arranging your child's environment as much as possible to prevent unnecessary conflicts before they happen.

Placing your child's toys at his eye level (in boxes or baskets while he is crawling, on low shelves when he starts to walk) will save him from having to cry when he wants to play with something new. If he constantly pulls the books off your lower bookshelves, start storing his own picture books there. If he loves to play with your dishwasher, plan to use dishwashing time as an exercise in learning cooperation, letting him help you load and unload the silverware and open and close the dishwasher door. You can plan ahead for a finicky eater by keeping a variety of his favorite easily prepared foods on hand and letting him decide what he'd like to eat for lunch that day. Taking him outside will be easier for everyone if you pack extra food in case he gets hungry and give him his nap before you go (or plan to bring him home before he begins to get sleepy). Of course, in some cases frustration can be a good thing (out-of-reach toys motivate babies to stand up!), but most of the time a little forethought will prevent many a nonproductive, exhausting battle.

LEARNING EVERY SECOND: HOW YOUR CHILD'S COMPREHENSION GROWS

Imagine what it must be like to be a twelve-month-old. Just as his body is bursting to move forward, his mind is making quantum leaps in its own development—taking in information like a sponge and literally reforming itself around the kinds of stimulation it receives. Where once he perceived only a chaotic jumble of color, light, and sound, certain reliable patterns have emerged. He has figured out such basic concepts as up and down, here and there, and the differences between people and objects but is only beginning to understand that a parent who leaves the room continues to exist, that a plate pushed to the edge of a table will fall off, that the baby he sees in the mirror is himself.

Each of these vital neurological advances, and many more, will occur in your child's second year, propelled by the phenomenal brain development that began before birth and continues at the same rapid pace until about age two. During this period, the brain expands more rapidly than at any other time of life. Its 100 billion neurons, only loosely wired for the processes of vision, speech, movement, and touch at birth, have been building synaptic connections ever since, creating a network of interactive parts that has transformed your watchful newborn. He is now an observant individual capable of understanding the world around him and acting on what he knows. His brain has grown physically as well, from one-fourth its adult size at birth to three-fourths of its full size by age two.

Between the ages of six and eighteen months, your baby's neurological net grows increasingly dense, until it contains approximately one and a half times more branches (used to transmit messages within the brain) than he could ever use as an adult. At this point, most of the branches are still unused. Recent research by a large number of experts, including Drs. Craig Ramey of the University of Alabama at Birmingham and Harry Chugani of Wayne State University in Detroit, has revealed that which branches become permanent and which ones die away in early childhood depends *almost entirely* on the quality of physical, emotional, and cognitive stimulation a child receives before the end of the third year. Once a neuronal passage is stimulated by experience, its connections are reinforced and it becomes stronger. The stronger it becomes, the more likely it is that it will spring into action the next time a similar experience occurs— and the more easily it will integrate the new information. This cycle of experience and neuronal integration is how learning takes place.

In other words, your one-year-old is a bubbling cauldron of pure human potential, perhaps never more open to learning than right now. It is both exciting and daunting to consider how great a difference you can make from now on in the quality of his inner world. By playing peekaboo, reading stories, and sharing nursery rhymes with your baby, you are not only having fun with him and deepening your emotional connection, but you're also literally improving the quality of his mind. This is especially important now, because, as we will see throughout this book, certain "critical windows" of neurological development open between ages one and two (in, for example, the areas of language and some aspects of emotional growth) that will never open quite as wide again.

A PARENT'S STORY
Mastering the Software

"I have to tell you about the major breakthrough I had last week about my daughter, Kendra, and what she's going through," Giselle, the mother of a thirteen-month-old in my parenting group, told me recently. "I had just bought a new computer with all this really great new software that I had to learn from scratch. So I set it up on the dining-room table and started practicing. Meanwhile, Kendra was playing on the floor nearby, or staggering around the house, or watching her brother Jared play with his toys, and it seemed like every fifteen seconds she started wailing. Either she was mad because Jared had left the room, or she was mad because he had a toy and she wanted it, or she was mad about something none of us could figure out. And there I was, trying to work with this software that I couldn't make go, and the harder I tried, the less it seemed to work.

"Then, in the middle of all this frustration, Kendra crawled over to me, pointed at the fruit bowl, and said, 'Orange!' I turned to her and yelled back, 'No!'

"Of course, she burst into tears, and I hated myself for yelling at her. *I sound just like a one-year-old,* I thought. And then it hit me like a bolt of lightning: *Of course I do. Kendra and I are going through exactly the same thing!* Her trying to figure out how to make me give her that orange was exactly like me trying to make a command work right on my computer.

Toddlers' newfound skills allow them to explore their expanding world in exciting ways.

"I was overwhelmed with sympathy for both of us. Believe me, next time she gets upset because she can't run after the dog or reach something she wants, I'll be more sympathetic. And I'll understand how happy she is when she finally accomplishes those things, too."

LEARNING THROUGH THE SENSES: THE IMPORTANCE OF PLAY

For a one-year-old, the world is a jumble of kaleidoscopic sensations, and all of his energy is directed toward piecing the fragments of sound, image, movement, texture, taste, and emotional expression into a satisfying picture of how the world works. Tell a one-year-old that you'll be back in a minute and he'll quite likely begin crying the moment you leave the room. Play peekaboo with him—letting his eyes register your appearance, disappearance, and reappearance—and he will eventually come to understand that when you go away, you *will* come back. Other concepts that a child this age must master can best be learned through sensory experience as well. Causality—the notion that a specific action leads to a predictable result—can be experienced by stacking two blocks and knocking them down, kicking a ball and watching it roll away, or (unfortunately) snatching a toy from a sibling and watching her cry. The one-year-old's obsession with imitation may have something to do with this need to learn through physical sensation. Mimicking a parent's vocalizations or a sibling's behavior tells a toddler more about that experience—how it feels, on many levels—than passively witnessing it ever would. Repeating the words or behavior over and over gives him the same sense of "learning by doing" that helps us adults learn most effectively, while providing a sense of comfort and predictability.

A love of sensory experience also feeds the one-year-old's explosion in language development. Just watch your little one babbling to himself in the morning before you pick him up out of his crib, and you will see that the physical pleasure of creating different sound combinations is a big part of his motivation for learning. Language gives him the satisfying feeling of control he so craves at this age. His first words are likely to be labeling words (nouns such as "doggie" and "ba-ba"), and in a very real sense, his ability to name an object is equivalent to "owning" or controlling it. By eighteen months, he may begin to incorporate labeling words with actions ("Truck go") and to relate an object to a place ("Truck here"). This mastery of language gives him a way to reach beyond his body for the first time, moving toward a more symbolic relationship with his world—a relationship that will also reveal itself in his new ability to pretend that a box is a house, a doll a baby, or Daddy's shoulders a horse to ride.

Meanwhile, though, it is important to understand how close the links are among your toddler's physical, cognitive, and emotional worlds. His block-stacking and ball-kicking pursuits help him not only to understand the concept of cause and effect but also to develop his gross-motor skills. The games of peekaboo that lead to a cognitive understanding of object (and person) permanence also provide the emotional reinforcement of warm, pleasurable parent-child interaction. Your awareness of these activities' invaluable bonuses can help you guide and support your child's emotional and social development throughout this period as effectively as you nurture his body and brain.

When rolling a ball back and forth to each other, you can talk about and demonstrate "taking turns." When you are coloring together and he wants your red crayon, you can give it to him while introducing the concept of sharing. Not all of these attempts to ground your child emotionally will "take" the first, second, or even third time, of course, but this is the age to begin experimenting with ways to help him understand and manage his emotions. In any case, as recent research causes scientists to push the age of comprehension back further and further toward infancy, it makes sense to introduce any concept just a little earlier than you think your child can understand it. At the very least, you'll be ready when he is.

THE TOY BOX
At Twelve Months

It is morning, breakfast is finished and Sam is crawling happily across the living-room floor. At the far end is his toy basket, and he can see his favorite toy—a plastic disk with brightly colored buttons that play animal sounds when you press them—sticking out over the edge. He reaches the basket, rises to his knees, and tugs on the toy until it comes free. It slips out of his hands and lands on the wooden floor with a loud, satisfying bang. Intrigued, Sam moves closer to the toy. He picks it up, then lets it drop again. *Bang!* Sam can feel the vibration from the noise in his legs and feet. He giggles and picks the toy up again. *Bang!* Sam continues picking up the toy and dropping it, fascinated by the relationship between the object's falling and the noise it makes. Every sense is busily taking in this information and feeding it to his curious brain.

Letting the toy drop to the ground one last time, Sam falls on top of it, exhausted. His arm accidentally pushes one of the buttons, and the toy emits a rooster's crow. "Sam!" says his mother's voice somewhere above him. "You made the rooster crow! That's wonderful!" Astonished, Sam looks from the toy to his mother's smiling face, to the toy again. He swings his arm down and hits another button. The toy meows like a cat. "Look," says his mother. "You made the cat meow." Amazed, Sam stares at the toy. A great number of connections—in the cognitive, emotional, and physical areas—are being stimulated in his brain. Soon Sam crawls away to look for other amusement. But the seemingly random, undirected play experience has not been wasted. Sam's brain will build on this experience of dropping something and watching it fall, of performing an action and receiving praise, of pushing a button and hearing a sound, and of hearing such words as "Look," "cat," and "meow"—moving him along in his development in a natural, pleasurable way.

MANAGING HIS WORLD: YOUR TWENTY-FOUR-MONTH-OLD

When you stop to consider how much your child is learning every single moment he's alive, a toddler starts to seem like a truly wondrous being. Draining as his enormous energy can be at times, frustrating as his determined "No!" or even his tantrums can be, it is impossible (in our calmer moments) not to admire him for his sheer determination and drive. It's been a very eventful year for Philip and for his parents, too, as they learned to deal with his frustration at his limited ability to control events, to communicate his feelings to others, or to make himself feel better. As his skills developed, his level of frustration decreased. As his parents got to know him better, they found ways to prepare for and deal with many of the difficult moments that did arise. Now, as his second birthday approaches, they are more relaxed as they watch him play, knowing that he is less likely to throw away a challenging toy in anger than to gesture at them to make it work, that he will use his past experiences to help him solve its mysteries, and that he knows that whether or not he can master the toy, he is a smart little boy.

As you read more about your child in the chapters that follow, keep in mind how exciting this period is for him. Support him in his admirable attempts to learn, develop, and grow. And be patient. Remember that your child is different from all others. He is not likely to follow exactly any developmental checklist put forth in parenting books and magazines

(including the timetable that follows, which is intended not as a "test" but as a general guide). In the end, the vast inconsistencies in the ways children grow are what keep them fascinating. So appreciate him as he is, and be glad that he can still—and always will—manage to surprise you now and then.

ADVANCES
Major Achievements in the Second Year

Here are a scattering of behaviors that parents often see at these ages. If your child doesn't demonstrate them at the time indicated, don't be alarmed. Think of these as new territory he will probably visit soon.

12 MONTHS   Stands alone

Responds to very simple commands

Indicates what he wants mostly with gestures

Plays alone when with other children

15 MONTHS   Tries hard to communicate

May walk with more confidence

May enjoy saying no

18 MONTHS   Likes to look at books

Displays increased vocabulary

Gets frustrated easily

21 MONTHS   Can climb stairs

Likes to help with household chores

Can carry out a simple plan

24 MONTHS   Can probably form two-, three-, or four-word sentences

Engages in basic pretend play

Is much more confident on his feet

FIRST-PERSON SINGULAR

In the next twelve months, your child's progress will amaze you, as he advances in walking, talking, feeding himself, and interacting with new friends. Take a moment now to fantasize about what sort of person is about to blossom from the seeds of personality you've already been observing. What will he be like—risk-taking and adventurous, sociable and chatty, curious and intense, shy and sensitive—more like his mother or his dad? What will he like to do most? How do you expect to structure his days? By writing down your ideas now, you can compare them to how you feel about your child twelve months from now, when you reflect on what an exciting time the two of you have just gone through.

READER'S NOTES

_____

_____

_____

_____

_____

_____

_____

_____

_____

_____

CHAPTER 2

Starting the Motor—My Physical Abilities

By the time she's two, she will be walking, feeding herself, punching buttons, hammering pegs, and opening every cabinet door in the house.

For weeks, twelve-month-old Tara has been cruising around the house on her own two feet, keeping one hand on a piece of furniture, the wall, or a friendly adult's pants leg as she experimented with walking upright. Rob and Liza, her parents, have pulled out the cameras half a dozen times already, convinced she was about to take her first unaided step, but each time Tara thought better of letting go of her support and turned back toward the coffee table or dropped onto her hands and knees. Last night would have been the perfect time for her to cross the walking threshold: Grandma, Granddad, and Rob's brother's family were all over for dinner and put a lot of energy into encouraging her to take a few steps across the room. Tara reveled in their attention—sitting on the floor, waving her hands, and chortling—without providing the expected "entertainment" in exchange. Tonight Rob and Liza sit slumped together on the couch, watching television, a little discouraged over Tara's progress, though neither one will admit it.

Meanwhile, Tara sits in front of her toy box in the corner of the living room, playing contentedly with a wooden hammer and pegs. If she senses her parents' suppressed frustration, she has no idea what's causing it.

Searching for another toy, she grasps the edge of the toy box and pulls herself to her feet. While she's digging around, she hears a pleasant tinkling sound and turns to see her mother lifting a glass of iced tea to her lips. The ice in the glass is what's making the soft, pleasant sound. It glistens as it moves around inside the glass. Tara is filled with an overwhelming desire to touch it.

She grunts to express her desire for the glass. Then, without thinking, she starts moving toward it. The ice continues to glisten tantalizingly inside the glass. By now Tara has walked as far as she can toward the couch without letting go of the toy box. She hesitates, looking from the box to the glass in her mother's hand. Then, just like that, she lets go.

"Liza!" Rob has glanced away from the television in time to see Tara take a first, tentative step. "Liza, look!" Liza watches, too, as Tara staggers forward again. The momentum of this second step sends her plopping back down to the floor. Her surprise is magnified by her parents' sudden, inexplicable explosion of applause, and she starts to howl. "You did it, Tara!" Rob shouts, rushing over to scoop her up. "Liza, where's the camera! I can't believe we left it in the dining room!" He gives her daughter a big hug, while she continues wailing—little realizing that she's just made a literal "first step" into the world of adult human beings.

Over the next year Tara will continue to develop and refine her walking ability—not all at once, and not in a smooth, regular sequence, but in uneven spurts of activity that will alternate and overlap with other advances. Soon, motivated by her parents' praise, her desire to examine objects that are otherwise out of reach, and her inner drive toward motor development, her first unsteady steps will progress to a wide-legged, sway-backed, staggering toddler's gait. By her second birthday her posture will have begun to straighten somewhat, her movements become smoother, and her feet taken her to practically every nook and cranny in the house in a constant search for new stimuli for her hungry mind. She will have learned to feed herself with a spoon, empty and fill containers, punch buttons, pull levers, hammer pegs, and open cabinets and drawers. So much of her parents' energy will be spent looking out for their child's safety as she plows ahead from room to room, sidewalk to playground, and parking lot to department store, grasping and manipulating any object within reach, that they'll no doubt marvel over that first-birthday lament, "I can't wait until she walks!" But even the weariest parent has to admire the tenacity with which the one-year-old moves forward through her environment, utterly determined to learn about every aspect of the world—and of her brand-new walking, learning, exploring self.

THE TOY BOX
At Twelve Months

Sonya has found her favorite new toy in her toy box—the plastic shape box Mommy gave her yesterday. She smiles and sits down on the floor with it, babbling to herself. She likes the rattling noise the shapes make inside. Mommy appears, says something in a pleasant voice, and opens the lid of the box. Delighted, Sonya holds up the box, then tips it over. The different-shaped plastic blocks fall out! *Wow—that was interesting.*

Before Sonya can investigate further, Mommy puts the lid back on and hands her one of the blocks. "Circle," Mommy says. She points to a round hole in the box. Frowning in concentration, Sonya tries to maneuver her hand toward the hole. After some trial and error, she manages to get the circle into the round hole. The nice noise it makes when it drops in and the happy sounds Mommy makes echo Sonya's feeling of satisfaction at having made her hand do what she wanted it to do.

Mommy hands Sonya another shape. "Square," Mommy says. Sonya confidently moves the square toward the round hole. But it won't go in. Sonya tries several times to solve this problem, but her fine-motor and cognitive skills aren't quite up to it yet. She smacks the box with the plastic square. Suddenly the muscles in her legs call to her. It's time to move on! Sonya pulls herself to her feet and toddles off. She'll learn more about shapes another day.

EXPLORING THE BODY: MOTOR ACHIEVEMENTS IN THE FIRST YEAR

It's tempting to date your one-year-old's walking life from the moment she took that first wobbly step, but in fact she's been developing the muscle control required for walking and other advanced motor skills since she first learned to sit up, if not before. At six to seven months, she managed to operate her stomach, leg, and upper-body muscles sufficiently to sit while propping herself with her hands. Sometime between seven and ten months, she was able to sit without props, freeing her hands to reach out for and grasp the things she wanted. Meanwhile, her spine began to straighten from the six-month-old's slump to the greatly improved posture of the older baby. Soon afterward she contrived to get both knees under her abdomen, push up off the floor, and start creeping or crawling—perhaps backward at first.

By her first birthday, her body and brain have developed to the point at which walking becomes her top priority, whether or not she's actually taken a step. Eating, sleeping, and even cuddling will take a backseat to her urge to move until she satisfies her now overwhelming desire. A skilled creeper-crawler, she will amaze you with the speed at which she can cross a room on hands and knees. But her skill on all fours doesn't impress her any longer. She is now obsessed with the drive to pull herself upright.

You will not be able to predict exactly when those first steps will occur, and they will not necessarily follow her ability to stand and to cruise the furniture in a regular, smooth progression. She may cruise for a couple of weeks before venturing forth without help, or she may move straight from crawling to walking. This uneven, almost jerky progress is typical of the way all of us humans develop new physical skills. An adult learning to ice-skate, for example, might actually start by crawling on hands and knees until he feels comfortable standing on the ice. Just staying upright is a challenge for a while. Then, at some unpredictable moment, he will begin walking awkwardly. Several practice sessions later, the skater will begin to learn to balance "naturally" and start to pick up speed.

Learning to walk presents exactly the same challenges for a one-year-old—and proceeds in the same bumpy, uneven manner. There is probably no need for concern if your child continues cruising for weeks or even months after her first birthday without ever accomplishing that first step. Late walkers are just developing according to their own inner schedule; sooner or later that step will come. Keep in mind that heavier babies, and those with older siblings, tend to walk later than others. Your child's need to focus on one skill may cause her to appear "stuck" for a while. This is perfectly normal. She may even fall back temporarily, crawling again when she'd already learned to stand. This probably just means she needs a rest— like a skater who stops and holds on to the railing for a moment before moving on.

Whenever she does start to walk, your baby will be extremely proud of her accomplishment. Her face will be wreathed in smiles as she looks to you for the approval she rightfully expects. In the weeks that follow, she will devote nearly all her energy to refining her primitive walking skills, even "practicing" walking in her dreams to the point where her muscle movements wake her up.

A PARENT'S STORY
Car-Seat Blues

"Running errands used to be a breeze with Marisol," Connie, mother of two, told me. "She'd fall asleep three minutes after I started the engine. The vibration would just put her right out." Now, though, Marisol was twelve months old, and Connie said that her daughter screamed every time she even heard the word "car."

It's easy to imagine how infuriating it must be for a one-year-old, whose deepest desire is to remain constantly on the move, to be buckled into a confining baby seat and forced to sit in a car for half an hour or longer at a time. "She kicks and screams the whole time I'm trying to close that buckle," Connie said, "even when I promise she'll just be there for a little while."

Connie wondered if her daughter was "acting spoiled" by screaming every time she rode in the car. She wasn't, of course— she was just acting normal. As I pointed out to Connie, trying to force a one-year-old to sit quietly in confinement is like trying to teach a cat not to purr. The best way to handle this unpleasant situation is to minimize the number of times you'll have to go through it. Consider how many stops you plan to make while doing your errands—and how many times you plan to take your toddler out of her seat and then (horrors!) put her back in. Is there any way to minimize the number of stops—by, say, walking instead of driving between two nearby stores, using the drive-through windows at banks, restaurants, photo developers, etc.— or perhaps skipping one or two errands until you can go alone?

When you do have to buckle her in, distract her from her horrible "I'm out of control" feelings by showing her a snack and telling her she can have it "as soon as you're in your seat." Keep a tape of her favorite songs in the car to play as you drive along, or sing to her and encourage her to join in. Some activities designed especially for car-seat use may be appropriate, as long as she can manipulate them on her own: busy books that fasten onto the seat, a plastic steering wheel that will make her feel as though *she* is driving the car, or a noise-making toy that she can hold. Remember, if you can turn car time into a fun experience *before* she starts to resent sitting in her seat, she may continue to look forward to riding around with you and not initiate the pattern of resistance that can make running errands so difficult.

Remember, though, never leave your child in the car unattended. Always take her with you, even if you are just dropping off a package at the post office. Don't take a chance with your baby's health or safety.

YOU CAN'T STOP ME NOW: LEARNING TO WALK IN THE SECOND YEAR

By fifteen months, your child may well be able to walk with relative ease even while holding something in her hands, though she continues to use a wide-legged gait and falls easily and frequently. Knowing how shaky her new skill still is, she's likely to drop down to her hands and knees and crawl when she's in a hurry. (I remember watching my own toddler, eager to pick up a ball and run, drop to her knees, put the ball in her mouth, and then crawl across the room at top speed.) This new ability to motor around means that the child is much better able to explore her world in multifaceted ways—reaching for and grasping new objects, climbing up and over things, and opening cupboard doors. Clearly, it also means she has many more opportunities to seriously hurt herself by falling or handling dangerous objects. It's time to fence off stairways, since she can probably crawl up them. Install baby locks on cabinets that contain dangerous substances, or move the substances to a cabinet that's out of reach. It's fine to use a playpen when you need to wash your hair, concentrate on a phone call, or otherwise be unavailable to keep her safe—as long as you "set her loose" afterward to continue satisfying her healthy urge to explore.

Rhythm and patterns of all kinds become increasingly interesting to one-year-olds as they continue to practice walking, climbing, and moving in other ways. Your child will find interruptions in rhythmic clapping very funny—as when you sing "Pop Goes the Weasel" or chant "This Little Piggy" and end with a tickle. As soon as she can walk easily, she's likely to climb onto your leg for a game of "This is the way the ladies ride" or onto your lap for a bounce on your knee. She'll also begin to move spontaneously to rhythmic music, expressing her pleasure in the beat by bouncing, swaying, and trying to sing a word now and then. This rhythmic involvement is important for enhancing such cognitive growth as the comprehension of sequence and time, as well as motor skills. You can encourage your little one's participation by joining in, moving joyfully to the music yourself.

By around eighteen months, your toddler will begin to exude a new confidence in moving her body. She will look more at ease as she stands and examines objects or walks toward a loved one. She will still stagger a bit and continue to fall frequently, but her movements will have become noticeably smoother and more deliberate than they were even three months earlier. At this point, her greatest joys will center on running (still stiffly, and just a little bit at a time), climbing and descending stairs (placing two feet on each step), and climbing into, up, and over any object in her path. Her movements are still mostly big ones (lugging, pulling, pushing). When she throws a ball while sitting, her legs will kick out at the same time. Her entire body is still involved in nearly every movement. Refinement will come later.

Don't expect her to direct her own activities consciously at this age. Ceaselessly wandering around, she tends to bump into objects at random, then start to investigate them. In fact, the eighteen-month-old's motto must be "Do before you think." She will run into the next room and then decide to explore it, instead of the other way around. She will put an object into her mouth and then decide whether or not she wants to taste it. Because of this do-first-think-later mentality, and because she's in al-most constant motion, it's still vital to monitor her activity with great care. It takes only an instant for her to pull on an electrical cord in an effort to learn about it or to make a big leap forward on the "down" escalator just because she feels like moving.

During this period—during her entire development, for that matter—your child will progress through each stage of growth largely through a process of trial-and-error experience. In other words, chances are excellent that she did not grab that electrical cord to aggravate you, but because she needed to find out what would happen if she did. Repetition—and experiencing minute variations with each repetition—is another one of a child's most powerful tools for integrating physical and other kinds of knowledge. Your toddler may run back and forth the length of the house fifty times in a given hour or bang on pots and pans for five minutes at a stretch—not to drive you crazy, as it sometimes seems, but because she needs to practice until she gets it right.

Vital as they are, these approaches to learning can truly test parents', caregivers', and other family members' patience during this year. It may help to look forward to the day—at around twenty-one months—when you first see how this sometimes maddening behavior has begun to pay off. By that time, your child will start to exhibit new smoothness and self-confidence in walking and running. The pleasure she has learned to take in her body will be apparent in her desire to run, dance, twirl, jump, and climb whenever she gets the chance. Her new skills will instill a healthy sense of independence that will expand as she enters her third year.

If the first steps she took toward you around her first birthday filled you with well-deserved satisfaction, her first steps *away* around her second birthday should make you feel equally proud. You have given her the room she needs to measure herself against the world and see what she (and it) is made of. She now has the confidence to move ahead on a more sophisticated level, comfortable with her body and with what she can make it do.

Walking Delays

It's difficult to remain calm when your one-year-old is still crawling long after her friends have begun walking erect. But, as I will emphasize throughout this book, the *rate* of development among one-year-olds varies widely, even if the *sequence* of steps is nearly always the same. There is probably no need for concern when your child has not begun walking by thirteen or fourteen months, if her other developmental skills seem to be on track and there is no family history of physical developmental problems. You may be able to spur her progress somewhat by regularly holding her hands and "walking" her to rhythmic music or nursery-rhyme chants in a fun, nonpressured manner. One thing to avoid: using a walker to encourage her to take her first steps. The American Academy of Pediatrics (AAP) strongly discourages the use of walkers because they are responsible for a huge number of accidents among five- to fifteen-month-olds (25,000 accidents in 1993). Walkers roll down stairs; tip over, causing children to hit their heads; and allow babies access to dangerous objects that parents had thought were out of their reach. In any case, the AAP reports, walkers have no effect on babies' walking development and may even delay it, since they prevent children from practicing the movements necessary to get to their feet and start moving on their own.

Certainly, if your child appears slow in several other areas of physical development and you have a "gut feeling" that something is wrong, monitor her progress (but don't panic), and call your pediatrician's office or mention your concerns at her next checkup.

Your pediatrician has probably been tracking her development all along, and chances are that the two of you can figure out together whether anything's wrong. Remember, you know your child better than anyone else does, and as with all other aspects of raising your child, your instincts regarding her physical development are a valuable tool, not to be discounted.

I CAN DO IT MYSELF:
FINE-MOTOR DEVELOPMENT

Though walking is a primary aspect of physical development this year, it's not the only way your child is growing. Fine-motor development—her ability to grasp and manipulate objects and control other aspects of movement—is phenomenal right now, helping her become almost as independent as she'd like to be. From the beginning, this development has been aided by advances in her movement skills. At age four months, when she was limited to lying on her back or sitting in her bouncy seat, she concentrated on learning to wave her hands, kick her legs, and hang on to objects that were handed to her. At seven to ten months, she could grasp and manipulate only objects that were within her reach while sitting up. At ten to twelve months, her crawling ability gave her better access to new objects, and her hands became increasingly active and helpful.

By her first birthday, her fast-speed crawling and hesitant first steps have given her more opportunities to refine her grasping and reaching ability, thus exploring her world in new ways. Now that she can grasp tiny objects between her thumb and forefinger, now that her hands have learned to grasp and release, she delights in comparing the textures of various objects and trying hard to figure out "how things work" in general.

The confidence that increased movement affords her extends to all other aspects of your one-year-old's life. At twelve months, she's likely to start being very demanding about wanting to do things herself. Often, she thinks she can do more than she can, and her unexpected failure proves very frustrating. Providing her with experiences at which she can succeed—allowing her to finger-feed herself, letting her "pretend" to feed

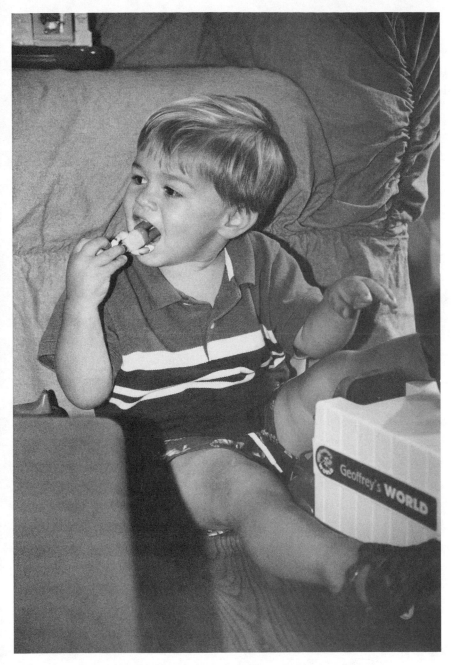

Safety is still a critical issue, as toddlers continue to explore objects with their fingers and their mouths.

herself with a spoon, cooperating with the seemingly endless games of drop-the-toy-and-make-Daddy-give-it-back, and showing her how to use fat toddlers' crayons—not only will further bolster her confidence but may lessen the number of outraged cries.

By age twelve months, your baby can form her hand around the shape of an object, such as a spoon or a marker, and she can tell if an object is out of reach. If you give her a ball, she can fling it awkwardly or roll it along the floor. She can wave bye-bye, and her continued involvement in old games such as peekaboo and patty-cake help her improve her hand-eye coordination, her ability to clap, and other skills.

At around fifteen months, your child will probably become fascinated by the process of emptying and filling containers—though she'll still be much better at the emptying part. Handing her a big bowl full of tennis balls (or any other objects big enough not to choke her) will keep her occupied for a surprisingly long time. This process of putting in and taking out will help her begin to understand the concept behind a shape box, if she has one; at this age she should be able to fit a round block into a round hole. Hammering pegs into holes (as with tool-bench toys) provides the same kind of satisfaction on a more whole-body level. Stacking blocks has also become great fun. Your child can probably stack at least one small block on top of another. It's a good idea to keep the toys out in the open, at eye level, so she can get to them easily when she's in the mood. Your child's enchantment with putting objects inside other objects will motivate her to help you put things away—though she may want to dump them right out again!

At eighteen months, your baby's ability to walk, grab, push, and pull has improved greatly, but her hand and arm movements are still a bit awkward. She still uses whole-arm movements in throwing a ball or playing with her toys. She often drops things. When she tries to turn the page of a book, she usually turns three or four instead. Still, her muscles are beginning to work together better. She can now build a tower of three or four small blocks, though she fusses when they fall over. She can pull a pull toy, but it's frustrating when it keeps tipping over. She can even use a spoon or fork, though she may still prefer her fingers.

During the last few months of this second year, your child's hand-eye coordination will continue to improve. She will experiment and learn to

Toys that both encourage physical interaction and show concepts are best for toddler learning.

fit plastic or wooden rings onto a spindle in order of size. She will be able to bring a full spoon to her mouth (sometimes right side up). She'll get better at helping you put the silverware, pots and pans, and books in their proper places. She'll also learn to be more efficient in her movements: When holding two objects, for example, she'll figure out how to store one under each arm in order to take a third. This gradual (though not necessarily regular) improvement in coordination and fine hand movements will increase through the third year, as she learns to throw a ball; string beads; cut with scissors; hold a cup of milk without spilling; pull on pants, shirt, and laceless shoes; and build an even taller tower of blocks. But the grace with which she moves and the skill with which she manipulates her small body are grounded largely in the experiences she has had this past year. Practice makes perfect for children as well as adults. The more opportunities she has to experiment with physical movement, with handling objects, and with self-care skills such as feeding and dressing herself, the more at ease she will become with her body and its place in the world.

Physics at Lunchtime

Mmm. Smells good. Naomi, fourteen months old, sits in her high chair, gazing at her plate of rice and chicken. *If I can just get my hand on it . . . There.* Naomi has a nice handful of chicken, but how can she get it to her mouth? *Hard to do—like holding my spoon without dropping it.* Concentrating hard, she moves her fist toward her face, using her arm like a crane. *Uh-oh!* She's knocked her sippy cup of milk to the floor.

Dad picks up the cup, puts it back on the tray, and says something to her daughter. Naomi smiles at him, though she doesn't understand her words. *Hmm,* she thinks. *Naomi make cup fall again . . .*

Her eyes wander to her hand. *Uh-oh! No chicken!* In her fascination with the fallen cup, she has let go of her food. *Get milk,* she decides, and slowly maneuvers her hands toward the cup, wholly engrossed in her task as her dad looks impatiently on.

I CAN GO ANYWHERE:
SAFETY CONCERNS

To the one-year-old, the world is a fabulous playground that begs to be explored, yet her concepts of what is and is not physically safe haven't yet developed sufficiently. For this reason, the second and third years are two of the most difficult in which to keep your little one safe. Speeding cars, steep stairways, candy-colored pills, and intriguing bottles in the cabinet under the kitchen sink all beckon, inviting her to touch, climb, taste, probe, and otherwise investigate. Since you can't watch your child every moment of every day for the rest of her life, the sooner you begin to teach her the "habits of mind" with which she can ensure her own safety, the better off she and you will be. Fortunately, young children are largely creatures of habit, so if you focus on just a few rules that can never be broken, your child will most likely accept them.

To this end, make sure that *every* time you go out walking, she holds an adult's hand before she crosses the street. Teach her *never* to touch the stovetop, because it may be hot. *Never* allow her to play with cleaning-fluid containers, even if they've been washed out and refilled with sand or water (use soda bottles instead). Don't assume that she will follow these rules on her own just because you've repeated them to her. You probably baby-proofed your home to a certain extent once she learned to crawl, covering electrical sockets, removing heavy and/or dangerous objects from coffee tables, etc. Now that she is walking, you will need to "raise the height" of baby-proofing to her eye, reach, and exploration level, installing baby gates, placing rugs or other padding under stairs, putting cushions under the crib when she starts trying to climb out, and installing lockable latches on kitchen and bathroom cabinets. Lots of parents suggest literally getting down to her level and looking around to discover all the tempting but dangerous or breakable items within her reach. (Did you remember the computer? Is there spare change lying around?) Remember, now she can get her hands on many more small objects that could choke her if she puts them in her mouth, and she is likely to do so. Keep a constant eye out for these objects and place them up high. The one-to-two-year-old doesn't worry about the consequences of climbing a ladder, popping a marble into her mouth, or toddling out into the street, so as the adult, you have to.

Q & A
Don't Touch or Can't Reach?

Q: My sister and I have a difference of opinion about how much parents should baby-proof their houses when their kids learn to get around on their own. My sister, who has a nine-month-old, has put every single breakable or dangerous thing out of reach in her house. I feel that my one-year-old needs to learn how to deal with these things and get to know what's fragile and what's dangerous, so I put only serious poisons like household cleaners out of reach and leave the rest. Which of us is right?

A: To a great extent, you both are. Baby-proofing works not only to protect your toddler from obvious dangers such as electrical sockets and bleach but also to allow your home life to proceed smoothly without repeated, avoidable minor crises. If your one-year-old has become so fascinated by the telephone that she can't resist constantly taking it off the hook, for example, moving the phone will prevent her getting into trouble constantly and your losing your temper. Later, you can demonstrate the phone's purpose by helping her call Grandma. In general, it's best to create as varied and rich an environment as possible for your child (including opportunities to learn how to handle some breakable objects), while protecting her safety and the family's peace of mind. So put away your favorite breakable objects, but leave out a few less precious and less dangerous things for her to practice with. In this way, she can learn while you can spend much less time saying no.

I TRY IT NOW:
LIVING WITH EXPERIMENTATION

As your child approaches her second birthday, she will become increasingly aware of the progress she has made in becoming an independent person, just like her older siblings, parents, and caregivers. This feels very good, and she will naturally want to augment that good feeling by acting as independently as possible. As parents, our job is to encourage this healthy drive toward independence without pushing too hard. It's a good idea to applaud your baby's efforts to feed herself with a spoon, for instance. It's not a good idea to *make* her use a spoon at every mealtime or to tell her she's acting like a baby because she decides she needs a break from practicing that skill and reverts to feeding herself with her hands. Keep in mind also that young children cannot develop fully without a great deal of trial and error, repetition, and just plain mess. It's unpleasant to have her throw her food on the floor on days when you're already feeling stressed, but it's an inevitable part of a one-year-old's growth.

The happiest parents, it seems, are those who accept the fact that a mess will occur and prepare for it by placing newspaper under the high chair, using plastic dishes with suction cups to keep them on the highchair tray, and keeping cleaning supplies nearby. By doing this, you free yourself to observe your child's progress and share in her delight over the new discoveries she's making amid the chaos. One mother of three whose home I visited had clearly devoted some thought to avoiding chaos in the playroom. She had arranged play areas and toy shelves at three different heights, so that the seven-year-old's toys were usually out of the three-year-old's reach, and the one-year-old could get to her own toys and no one else's. Imagine how many potential conflicts she eliminated with that single design effort! You will find that your child's life is increasingly full of such opportunities to maximize pleasure and minimize stress. Take advantage of them.

Just as there's no point in resenting the inevitable messes and repetitions of babyhood, it doesn't make much sense to confront head-on a little person so determined to control her environment. Maddening as it can be to watch the clock tick while your determined eighteen-month-old struggles to put on her own shoes, such attempts at self-sufficiency are a healthy, admirable, and utterly necessary part of growing up. The solution to these "I can do it myself!" dilemmas lies in what I call "the power of Velcro": making it as easy as possible for your child to manage her environment, so that she feels in control while you still manage to get to work on time. Keeping her snack food and dishes in a lower cabinet at her height, providing clothes with few buttons or snaps, placing a step-stool in the bathroom so she can stand at the sink while you help wash her hands—these are all ways to help your child feel independent while allowing you to get through the day efficiently. No, you are not spoiling her by waiting for her to manage on her own. You are giving this new human being the room she needs to grow.

EASING THE WAY
A Work Space of Her Own

If she hasn't already, your fifteen-month-old will soon enter her first age of perceived self-sufficiency, in which she believes she can do practically everything herself and will certainly insist on doing so. Since healthy self-confidence and a can-do attitude are positive qualities to encourage in any child, this might be a good time to provide your little one with a table and chair just her size. Sitting at a table enables her to play "office," to draw, to play with clay, and to manipulate stuffed animals more comfortably. By pulling up your own chair (or better yet, sitting on one that's her size), you can keep her company, observe her daily development in a thousand fascinating ways, and reinforce her sense of herself as a "big girl" who "works hard," just like the grown-ups in her world. As she practices with the fat crayons she probably prefers (you can tape down the edges of the paper to make it easier for her), you may notice that she can now imitate a stroke you make. Reading a picture book together, you may be surprised to see her try, and sometimes succeed, in turning a page. Her table can also be used for solitary snacks, where she can have her meal on a tray, practice holding her cup in both hands, and otherwise rehearse for the big-girl years ahead.

LOOK—I DID IT!: STEPPING INTO A WIDER WORLD

It's been a year since Tara took her first steps, surprising herself at least as much as her parents. Now, on her second birthday, she runs from room to room with all the energy and excitement of a growing girl. Over the past twelve months, her body has developed from that of a baby to that of a young child. Thanks to her parents' efforts to let her "do it herself" as much as possible, her coordination has improved; her gait is smoother and more efficient than it was just three months ago; she is able to feed herself, drink from a cup, and scribble with a crayon; and her precious sense of independence and self-sufficiency has been bolstered by her new (sometimes still flawed) ability to tend to herself, obtain what she needs, and explore her world. Her emotional and cognitive gains have been well served by her developing body—as her mom and dad know from having watched for signs of progress. She is a unique individual now, poised to take her first giant steps into the exciting world just outside her front door.

Fine- and Gross-Motor Achievements in the Second Year

12 MONTHS   Stands alone

May take a few steps

Stacks two blocks

Grasps and releases objects more easily

15 MONTHS   Walks with staggering gait

May like to climb

Holds a crayon

Turns pages of book

18 MONTHS   Walks; perhaps runs and jumps

Climbs more easily

Needs a hand going up stairs

Pulls toy while walking

Likes fitting shapes into matching holes

May try to draw with crayon

21 MONTHS   Runs faster

Squats frequently

Needs a hand going down stairs

Throws more accurately

Enjoys scribbling and finger painting

24 MONTHS   May climb and descend stairs alone

Is much sturdier on feet

Likes to dance

Can stack five or more blocks

May show preference for one hand

FIRST-PERSON SINGULAR

Now, while the issues of physical development are fresh in your mind, take some notes about your child's latest advances in areas relating to movement and other activity. How is her mobility changing? Is she attempting to feed herself? If you have a photograph or videotape of her six months ago, look at it and write down some of the ways in which her skills have advanced since then. How is her behavior different from that described in this chapter? How is it the same? What do her physical strengths and weaknesses seem to be at this time? What is her most exciting accomplishment so far? What do you really look forward to seeing her do next? If possible, videotape her now, crawling, walking, eating, and playing, so you can monitor her changes next year.

Remember, it isn't necessary to actively play with your child every moment you're in her company. Often, it's just as important to step back and observe quietly. These moments of observation can greatly increase your understanding and help you work with her more effectively in the future.

READER'S NOTES

_____

_____

_____

_____

_____

_____

_____

_____

_____

_____

_____

_____

_____

_____

_____

_____

_____

CHAPTER 3

Thinking for Myself—My Cognitive Development

During the first three years, a child's environment literally helps build his brain.

When Leah was pregnant, she had dreamed that her son Craig's first birthday would be just like this: a sunny July afternoon with family and friends gathered in the backyard to celebrate. While the guests help arrange the gifts and peek in at the birthday cake in the kitchen, Leah sits on the back porch with Craig, blowing bubbles so he can watch them waft away on the breeze. Craig's round eyes track each floating orb with utmost seriousness. Each time a bubble bursts, his mouth makes a little O shape, his brow furrows, and he ducks his head to search for it. Leah laughs. "Look at this," she says to her husband, Jerry, who is videotaping the two of them. "Craig can't seem to get the idea that the bubbles are gone."

A friend calls Leah inside to help her set up the refreshments table. Leah leaps up, hands the bubble paraphernalia to Jerry, and runs inside. Behind her, Craig, who has been balancing unsteadily on his two chubby feet, falls back onto his bottom in surprise. *Where has Mommy gone?* his stunned gaze seems to say. *Has she disappeared forever, like the bubbles?* Craig stares at the empty space where his mommy just was. His eyes fill with tears and he starts to cry but stops the moment Mommy comes back to check on him.

It is sometimes very difficult for us adults to comprehend how a one-year-old views the world—especially since that view evolves constantly as he moves through this dynamic year. In this chapter we will examine your child's growing understanding of object permanence—the knowledge that people and objects continue to exist when they're out of his sight, his sense of where he is in space, and his concept of the passage of time. All of these concepts will be tested and refined as he becomes able to move about with greater ease, communicate more freely with others, and otherwise explore his world. The quality and variety of his encounters will largely define how complex and rich his thinking becomes. Gazing at bubbles is one of thousands of ways he might ponder the concepts of "here" and "not here." Your own natural coming and going is another. One of the greatest satisfactions—and responsibilities—of this year of parenting lies in providing your child with as wide an array of stimulating situations as possible and watching his understanding increase at a truly astounding rate.

NEW KNOWLEDGE ABOUT THE DEVELOPING BRAIN

Until recently most scientists believed that a baby's brain structure is for the most part determined by his genes, that it is virtually complete by the time he is born, and that this "inherited" aptitude determines in very large part how the child will interact with the world. Most of these assumptions were derived indirectly from animal research and observation and from interpretation of human behavior. As we know now, earlier scientists quite often underestimated how the brain works. Over the past few decades, new uses of noninvasive brain-imaging technologies, such as the positron emission tomography (PET) scan and magnetic resonance imaging (MRI), have allowed researchers to actually watch the brains of infants and children in the process of learning. These amazing windows into the working brain have created an explosion of new knowledge about human brain development—and have proven unequivocally that environment plays a much greater role in determining a child's intelligence quotient (IQ), emotional state, and destiny than scientists had ever imagined.

In other words, during his first three years, your child's environment literally helps build his brain.

When your infant was born, his brain consisted of a jumble of neurons, most of them still waiting to be woven together into a fully operational mind. Some of this wiring had been accomplished through the genes, a little more was created via messages from the mother's hormones, and still more was the result of the sounds, rhythmic movements, and other "environmental" influences in the womb. After birth, the environmental input to the brain increased astronomically. Each new sight, sound, personal encounter, touch, and smell created a new connection in your child's developing neural web. The more often an experience was repeated—the more times your baby reached out for his rattle and grasped it, for instance—the more likely it was that the related "brain connections" would be reinforced and made permanent.

Even now, at twelve months, the building of your child's brain is far from complete. During this year, he will learn most of the fundamental concepts that allow us to move through the world easily—that objects can be hollow or solid, that containers can be full or empty, that one event can lead to another in a predictable sequence, and so on. To a large extent, these facts must be learned through interaction with the environment; they do not just appear in the brain through genetic programming. This is why it is so important that your child be exposed to as wide a variety of stimulation as possible (without overdoing, of course) during this year. Each of the physical, emotional, and intellectual experiences he has during these twelve months will affect to some degree the way his brain will be wired for the rest of his life.

This does not mean that the absence of any single experience or learning opportunity (say, playing with a shape box) will make a crucial difference for your child, but a general absence of stimulation in a particular area (practically no talk about shapes or no opportunity to categorize objects by shape) can certainly hold him back. The *timing* of these experiences is important also. Certain types of stimulation are much more effective at certain times than at others. Dr. Janellen Huttenlocher of the University of Chicago has repeatedly demonstrated that a child who is spoken to a great deal and allowed to practice responding during his first two years is more likely to develop good language skills. On the other hand (as twenty years of research by Drs. Alan Sroufe, Byron Egeland, and others at the University of Minnesota has shown), a child who is abused or emotionally neglected very early in life may never fully develop a sense of empathy or secure attachment, and this can translate into problem-solving difficulties, relationship and school problems, and other cognitive deficits as the child grows.

Neurologists call these prime-time opportunities *critical periods.* They are the developmental reason your child suddenly becomes so focused on mastering a particular skill such as walking, communicating through language, or strengthening emotional attachments. Though of course it is never too late to help a child improve his ability, children learn best when caregivers take note of where their attention is focused and support their learning in that area *at that time.* Therefore, general checklists of a one-year-old's developmental interests and achievements (such as the one at the end of this chapter), are much less important in helping your child learn than are your own observations of his current interests.

A PARENT'S STORY
Setting the Stage

"Okay, I admit it. I'm an ambitious mom, and I know it's gotten in the way of helping my kids sometimes," a colleague said over coffee the other day. "With my older son, Andrew, I truly bordered on the ridiculous—reading to him while he sat on the potty during toilet training, introducing him to toys that were designed for children years older than he was. In one sense I don't think it was energy wasted. At least Andrew knew that I loved him and that I cared a lot about what he thought and did. But the fact was, his brain wasn't ready to try to recognize the letters of the alphabet on a page, for instance, when he was eighteen months old. He was interested in stacking blocks at that time. Now I realize that back then he needed to learn about balancing objects, not about how to read.

"With Cass, my daughter, I've tried to do things another way—letting *her* decide when it was time to learn something. I knew I couldn't predict exactly when she'd be interested in what activity, and I was busier now with two kids, so I couldn't follow her around every minute to find out. Sometime around her first birthday I decided to set up the house so that she could play with what she wanted when she needed it. I put a sandbox in the backyard, a hammer and pegs in her little play space, and some books with pictures of characters she knew and liked on her bookshelf. My house looks like a little Montessori classroom now, but I really think it's better letting her choose her 'lessons' instead of my forcing them on her. She learns when she's ready—and that's the best way to learn."

YOU'VE COME A LONG WAY, BABY: NEUROLOGICAL ACHIEVEMENTS

"It's endlessly fascinating to me, trying to figure out how Emily's brain works," a mother in my parenting group mentioned the other day. "You can see how it develops from the way her behavior changes month to month, or sometimes even from day to day." It's true. You can gauge pretty accurately where your child is in his developmental sequence simply by watching how he behaves. Nearly everything a one-year-old does literally expresses his "state of mind" at that particular moment. If he focuses intently on eye contact as you play peekaboo with him, and looks concerned when your hand covers your eyes, he's at a very basic level of attention. If he giggles with delight when you disappear behind your hands, wait a few seconds, and then reappear, he's at a distinctly more sophisticated stage. As he gets up on two feet, opens a drawer, and dumps out the contents on the floor, he's moved toward knowing that objects exist even when they're out of sight.

Of course, this process of actively studying his environment did not begin on his first birthday; its pace has simply quickened now that he has greater physical opportunities to access new information. From the first day of life (and even before), he has been busily processing the data he receives through his senses and through interaction with the people and objects within his reach. As an infant, when his reach was obviously very limited, his learning focused for the most part on repeating actions that first occurred accidentally (or that you instigated for him). He first noticed his hand because it happened to pass in front of his face, for example; only after he noticed it did he begin trying to put it into his mouth. Between eight and twelve months, as he became able to grasp things while sitting and to crawl, his interest turned to repeating actions that created intriguing sights or sounds—shaking a noisy toy, for instance, or making "ba-ba-ba" sounds that tickled his lips and felt good in his mouth.

By his first birthday, your child's increased range has allowed him to begin behaving in more actively experimental ways, varying his actions and noting their effect on his environment. This is the age when he enjoys punching a variety of buttons on a plastic toy and watching different objects pop up. As the year unfolds, he will also enjoy experimenting on you—spinning the knobs on the stereo, for example, and looking to see how you react.

As your baby's understanding of the world increases and his brain continues making new connections, an important change takes place in his thinking sometime between eighteen months and two years. He becomes capable of thinking about something without its actually having to be there. This new ability to "think symbolically"—to picture playing with his ball without having just seen the ball right there in front of him—means that he will be able to cook up more predicaments to get himself into, because he can imagine scenarios and plan ahead a little. But it also means that he might avoid pinching his hand in the cupboard door because he can remember how much it hurt last time he did that, or can even generalize from the time he caught his finger in the toy box. Your toddler's developing language ability is a great help in enabling him to frame these concepts and scenarios in his mind. In the second half of the second year, his symbolic thinking and language abilities combine with great strides in imaginative play, empathy, and a host of other vital skills to bring him to an entirely new level of comprehension.

Q & A
Hearts and Minds

Q: I have been taking my fifteen-month-old child to the same child-care center since he was eight months old. It's a small center, and fortunately the turnover is very low. My son has made some good friends among the child-care workers, and I think he feels very loved and secure there. However, I wonder whether he's getting enough intellectual stimulation. The staff are very good about holding the kids on their laps, cuddling them, and so on, but I don't really see much "teaching" going on. My question is, Should I look for a more stimulating environment or leave him where I feel he's loved?

A: You are the only one who can decide whether your child would do better in another situation. And naturally, all parents who work outside the home dream of finding a caregiver who is both nurturing and stimulating for their children. When making your decision, though, there are some developmental facts about children this age that you might want to keep in mind. First, studies have shown that children this age learn best—that is, their brains develop most efficiently—when the learning takes place in the context of secure, close relationships. Your one-year-old may be more open to learning where he is than with a new, unfamiliar, and possibly less nurturing caregiver. Second, much of what a child needs most to learn between twelve and twenty-four months— rock-bottom concepts including the dependability of loved ones, the predictability of daily routines, the near-certainty that when he communicates to another person the person will respond—can best be instilled through relationships that stay as stable as possible. This is not to say that a change in child-care arrangements would necessarily be a poor choice. But talk to the caregivers about their methods first to be sure your assumptions about them are correct. Visit the center at various times of day, so you don't just see the kids during rest time or lunch. And don't discount the neurological benefits of loving friendship. You can always make a point of "stimulating his brain" during your own time with him at home.

OUT OF SIGHT, OUT OF MIND:
OBJECT PERMANENCE

For the very young infant, the world is less like a movie than like a photo album—a series of snapshots that seem only vaguely related. Infants focus on and comprehend what they can see *right now,* paying little or no notice to what has passed or what is coming. If an object moved out of your three-month-old's range of vision, he immediately forgot about it. If your five-month-old dropped a toy, he was perfectly happy to accept a replacement. Likewise, babies up to about six months of age are often quite complacent about being left with a caregiver. Once Mommy or Daddy has left the room, the infants' minds are fully occupied with the person who has taken the parent's place. As with other aspects of babies' cognitive development, the age at which researchers consider children able to begin to understand that an object continues to exist even when they can't see it has been pushed back a number of times (due mainly to more sophisticated tests devised by child-development researchers) and is now believed to be at around six months.

In any case, by age eight to twelve months, a typically developing baby will search for a toy if you take it from him and hide it within reach. If you move the toy to another hiding place while he is watching, he is likely to look for it in the first hiding place rather than the second, unless the time between hiding and searching is very short. By twelve to sixteen months of age, he will look for the toy in the new hiding place—but only if he saw you move it. Only after his eighteenth month or so will he be able to recall his previous experiences with this game and look for the hidden toy even if he didn't see you hide it. Psychologists call these actions "displacements," but such appearances and disappearances are an important part of your child's everyday experience.

Trying experiments like the one above with your child can be fun and interesting for you both. It is amazing how clearly you will see the progress your little one makes as you experience the same situation together from one week or month to the next. While on an airplane recently, I watched an eighteen-month-old passenger demonstrate his own progress splendidly. The little boy sat by the window, the mother was in the middle seat, and a stranger sat by the aisle. At one point during the flight, the stranger left his seat. Naturally, the toddler's eyes lit up—he saw this as an opportunity to escape into the aisle, giving his stifled, motor-driven body a chance to explore. Unfortunately for him, his mom (who naturally wanted him to stay where he was) blocked his way to the aisle with her legs. She held up a toy to try to distract him, but her little one was clearly not satisfied with that.

How would he solve this problem? I wondered. At twelve months, he could have done nothing about it but push harder on her leg. He wouldn't have been able to plan an escape strategy in advance and then carry it out. Nor would he have been able to remember similar situations well enough to draw on those experiences for help. Pretending to read a magazine, I watched, fascinated, as the toddler took the toy from his mother, then tossed it gleefully into the aisle. Quickly, he checked his mother's face for her reaction.

How clever! Now his mother either would have to let him go into the aisle to get the toy or get up and get it herself, thus moving her legs and enabling him to escape. Clearly, his mother was exasperated by his behavior, but it was all I could do not to rush over and tell her what a bright and creative son she had. In just a few months, no doubt, he would try to talk his mother into letting him go (an even better solution than this one, which was foiled when another passenger simply handed the toy back to Mom), but in the meantime he had used every neural connection he had to solve the problem at hand. Parenting can feel like a thankless chore on many, many occasions, but at least we can sit back and marvel sometimes at how cleverly our children work to control their worlds and how impressively their brains develop to help them.

LEARNING BY DOING: FROM IMITATING TO CREATING

If the young child's journey of discovery leads from observation to imitation, experimentation, and finally symbolic thought and creativity, your one-year-old is already surprisingly far down the road. With months of more or less silent observation and study behind him, he has already begun imitating your sounds and actions with increasing skill. As you reward his attempts to behave "like a big boy" with smiles, hugs, and praise, his longing to be just like you increases exponentially. By the time he is around twelve to fifteen months, his desire to follow you out of the room is almost irresistible, he insists on feeding himself the way his big sister does, and he struggles daily to converse successfully with his sitter, no matter how long it takes.

This determination to do the things his caregivers and family members do is the fuel behind much of his neurological development and is the reason babies and toddlers learn better from those who love them than from strangers. At twelve months, he will watch you pour sugar into the sugar bowl and want to do that himself. Later, in the sandbox, you will show him how to pour. His delighted repetition of this motion that is "just like Dad's" will lead to all kinds of learning—about the characteristics of various material substances, about gravity and weight, about "empty" and "full," and so on. As the months pass, he will experiment with various ways of pouring sand, filling the sand bucket over and over and over, each time emptying it and stomping on the pile he's made. Still later, he'll concoct schemes to build a sand pile somewhere else in the yard and actually carry out his plans. By age two, he might direct you to do it and clearly communicate his disapproval if you don't comply. Without the initial drive to imitate that you can spot in the last half of the first year and the insistence of trying things out for himself, none of this learning would take place.

Q & A
Who Teaches Best?

Q: My son, Jonathan, is eighteen months old and an incredible mimic. Whatever he sees my husband or me doing, he has to try to do it, too. We've been able to use "copycat" tendencies to teach him all kinds of behavior patterns and new ideas.

Lately I've been thinking about arranging for a child-care situation for him so I can start working again. The problem is, I can't decide between hiring an in-home caregiver just for him or placing him in the group child-care center in our neighborhood. Is it better for him to spend most of his time five days a week observing and imitating an adult caregiver or other children his age (who might introduce him to negative behaviors and might not teach him much that's new)?

A: Imitation is a powerful, ever-present way in which children learn. The fact is, no matter where you place your child for care, he will imitate and learn much from others. The critical issue then, is not *whom* he will be imitating but the *quality of nurturing* and the *variety of activities* to which he will be exposed. A caregiver who takes him to the grocery store or to play with other children in the playground, or one who simply creates exciting play opportunities in your yard (bubbles, Play-Doh, music) can be a wonderful provider of stimulation and fun. In a center, as you point out, your son is guaranteed to have lots of peer interaction—with positive and negative behaviors galore to imitate—but odds are he won't form as exclusive a relationship to the caregiver, who needs to divide her time among several busy toddlers.

When deciding on the best child-care arrangement for Jonathan, consider the following: Does he have other opportunities to spend time with other children—for example, on weekend visits with family? Is he sensitive to overstimulation, which groups of children invariably provide? How well does he handle transitions, such as a change in caregiver or location? Has he already formed strong attachments to other adults in his life (so that he doesn't particularly need more such attachments now)? Which child-care arrangement will be less stressful (emotionally and financially) for your family?

Since research shows that quality of child care is the key ingredient, focus your decision on what matters most to your child at this point in his life, and most to you as a parent, and you will no doubt find a situation in which your child will thrive.

LANDMARKS IN THE WILDERNESS:
THE SENSE OF SPACE AND TIME

Have you ever gotten lost while driving through a part of town you didn't know? If so, you know that bewildering sense of moving aimlessly through unknown territory, searching for landmarks that will point the way. As soon as you find one building you know, you feel considerably more at ease. After that, a second landmark seems to appear more quickly. Then a third—until you know right where you are, and your confidence returns.

This is one way of imagining what the world might feel like to a very young child as he ventures forth on his hands and knees—and, eventually, his two feet—into the vast and mysterious external world. Just one "landmark"—his mother's presence, for instance—can provide him with enough confidence to venture a little further out into the unknown. As he explores, seeking new knowledge, another person or object becomes familiar to him, and then another and another. The more known objects and people fill his space, the more his world becomes defined—and the more confident he becomes that he can continue exploring further without undue risk, though he will still check his landmarks occasionally.

Your child must identify not only physical landmarks but cognitive ones as well. He must familiarize himself with a number of "obvious" laws of physics that affect the world he is exploring but that don't appear obvious to him at all. Having already begun to sense the fact that space exists in three dimensions, the nine- to twelve-month-old crawls to the kitchen cupboard to discover for the first time that objects often have an inside and an outside, that they can be hollow or solid. By twelve months, he has become fascinated by the idea of putting something inside something else. At around fifteen months, he will understand how to stack one block on top of another. By eighteen months, he will clearly comprehend "up" and "down," "open" and "closed," and such sentences as "Where's Duncan? There he is!" By the end of his second year he will understand "big" and "little" as well as "all gone." Each of these new concepts is a welcome landmark helping to make your child's world more predictable and comprehensible. The more landmarks he can rely on, the more confident he will feel about seeking out new information.

A baby's sense of time is "bumpy" in ways very similar to his awareness of the space around him. To a six-month-old, time passes not like a flowing river but in an endless series of milliseconds, each separate and distinct from the moments before and after. There is not really a concept of time other than the present. That is one reason it is often easier to leave a baby in the care of a sitter at that age. He isn't quite able to get his mind around the idea that once you were here and now you're gone— much less understand that you'll be back in four hours. By twelve to eighteen months, your baby has begun to develop at least a minimal sense of both cause and effect and immediate sequences of events. That is, he is aware that if he drops a toy, someone is likely to give it back to him, or that if he holds his arms up to Daddy, he will be picked up himself. These "bumps" in his temporal landscape are like landmarks he can return to again and again. If the expected sequence doesn't happen, his confidence is shaken, and he may start to cry or withdraw. His sense of time's progression has been violated.

As he gains experience during the first half of his second year, your child's collection of landmarks increases; he is able to remember and predict sequences of events that occur over a longer period of time. By eighteen months, he understands that the arrival of bathtime means that bedtime is approaching. Mommy's arriving home means it will soon be time to eat. As with spatial landmarks, these met expectations increase his confidence tremendously and give him a greater sense of control. In general, though, when outside the framework of daily routine, a toddler this age still lives in the moment. Saying he can go to the park "tomorrow" or that you'll be off the phone "in a minute" doesn't mean the same thing to him as it does to you.

The concept of "later" does begin to seep in as your child approaches his second birthday, however. By now, he has heard you say you'll give him another cup of milk "in just a second"—and then received it—often enough to at least begin to understand that the milk will eventually arrive. But even by age two, it is still hard for him to conceive of time in the abstract. It is still more effective to ground your comments in terms of concrete actions. Saying, "First we'll put on your coat. Then I'll take you to the playground" is clearer than "We'll leave in ten minutes, okay?" The two-year-old's concept of time is still somewhat bumpy, in other words— defined more by sequences of events than by a smoothly progressing clock.

By the end of the second year, you will be astounded at how far your child has come in his understanding of what his environment consists of, how it works, who is in it, and what his place in it is. His transition from determined explorer, to frustrated beholder of all he doesn't yet understand and can't yet do, to a stronger, smarter, and infinitely more capable twenty-four-month-old is truly astonishing. Providing him with reliable landmarks on his journey toward self-sufficiency is one of the greatest gifts you can give him.

A BABY'S-EYE VIEW
"Go Home!"

It is almost lunchtime, and fourteen-month-old Eugene is shopping with Lisa, his mom, at the mall. He feels his tummy rumble. *Hungry. High chair.* He looks around. The high chair is not here. He feels panicky—his tummy hurts! He starts to cry.

"I know, it's lunchtime," Lisa murmurs, glancing at her watch. She's irritated with herself for forgetting the snack bag, and her annoyance can be heard in her voice. "Just ten more minutes, okay, Eugene? We have to get some sheets at Sears, and then we'll go to a restaurant."

Mommy mad. Tummy hurts. Crackers! Eugene cries even harder.

His loud cries force his mother to stop and look at him. She realizes that this violation of the expected sequence—hunger to food—has really upset him. She doesn't have any crackers, but . . .

"Okay, Eugene," Lisa says, trying to keep her impatience out of her voice. "Here's your teddy." She winds it up, and its familiar melody starts to play.

Eugene hugs the stuffed bear. It smells good, feels good. The music and Mommy's calmer tone of voice comfort him. For now he forgets about the crackers.

A little later, Eugene and his mom enter the restaurant. Mommy says something to the lady. He smells the food. *Hungry!* He heads for a chair just as the lady brings menus and a pack of crackers for him. His physical need for food—and his cognitive need for predictable sequence—are both about to be satisfied, and thanks to Mom's ability to think on the fly, his need for comfort was met in the meantime.

PEEKABOO!: THE IMPORTANCE OF PLAY

"I wonder sometimes if I'm doing everything I can for Hanna," I overheard a mom say at the clinic one day. "I mean, she's nearly two already, and all she ever seems to do is hang around the house and play. I like hanging out with her, but I wonder if all the other parents in the neighborhood have started taking their kids to art classes or working with flash cards or something."

It can seem a little endless sometimes, as your child's second year progresses, to see him puttering about the house, happy as a clam but not obviously *doing* anything constructive. One minute you might find him scribbling on a pad of paper with the fat crayons you've provided; the next he might be tasting the crayon or squashing it beneath a block or sticking it into a ball of clay to see what happens. *Is this serious?* you ask yourself. *Can he possibly be learning anything?* The answer is yes, absolutely. For a toddler, play is work, and it is quite a serious matter. Your child may look as if he's just fooling around with a crayon, but he's actually gaining invaluable experience about the relative strength and plasticity of various objects while refining his motor skills! Every activity he's doing voluntarily must be teaching him something, or he wouldn't do it.

On the other hand, there are specific ways you can use your little one's love of play to extend his knowledge and reinforce those neural connections that will enrich his thinking. As you know, by the time he is one, your child will have become capable of moving beyond simple repetition in his play. He will be able and eager to expand his horizons through experimentation, constantly seeking new variations on experiences he has had before. This act of expanding on previous experience is the key to both pleasurable play and efficient learning. Encourage it whenever possible. Instead of stacking rings on the spindle with him the same way every time, encourage him to try stacking the rings without the spindle to see what happens. When they topple over, ask, "What else can we do with the rings?" Maybe you can string them on a shoelace or toss them

Note the joy on this toddler's face when he is in charge of this tried-and-true game of peekaboo.

into the toy box one by one. Narrate what you're doing: Name the color of each ring as you stack them, count how many you've stacked, or talk about which one is biggest and which smallest. Or have your child rub the rings with his fingers, note their texture, then rub the carpet he's sitting on—and invite him to compare the two.

All of this new information taken in through the senses will start those thousands of neurons firing away. He will add the new input he's just received to what he already knows, and make connections that will prepare him for even greater understanding the next time. The idea is always to start where the child is in his play and then "push the envelope" just a little, leading him ahead one step after another in the learning game.

What kinds of games does a one-year-old like to play? As always, you can best find out by observing your own child and following his lead. Keep in mind that it isn't necessary to have a large number of toys to keep your toddler occupied. Not only can he find a nearly infinite variety of ways to play with a limited number of toys, but most objects in his environment look like "toys" to him. He's as happy (or even happier) banging pots and pans on the kitchen floor as he is hitting a toy drum.

This is a good thing, because children this age tend to spend only brief periods with one object before moving on to another. In general, the one-year-old will use objects in play much as you use them in real life: He'll pretend to brush his hair with your brush (probably holding the brush upside down), whack on things with a toy hammer, and so on. As the year progresses, he'll increasingly partake in "symbolic" play—rocking a doll or pretending to drink from an empty cup. As his brain grows more complex, so will his pretend play. By his third year, he may insist that a wooden block is really a race car or that he is a horse and you are the horse's mommy or daddy.

The one-year-old particularly enjoys any game that involves being face to face or having physical contact with those he loves—such as peekaboo, "This Little Piggy," and acting out favorite stories together. Even when he can't perform all the parts of the game, you can see how focused he is on taking in information by the way he studies your face. Watch how delighted he is when you smile and tickle him at the end of "This Little Piggy," just as he'd predicted you would. Now try playing the game without the expected smile and tickle, and see how surprised he looks.

He will probably try to get you to perform the game correctly—maybe by vocalizing—demonstrating his earliest problem-solving skills. Reward him with a new game of "This Little Piggy" and a bigger tickle for his trouble!

As mentioned earlier, studies have shown that toddlers' play is especially productive when a baby's parents, other caregivers, or siblings participate. The pleasure of interacting with loved ones motivates them to pay more attention to what's going on. Children's play tends to last longer when parents join in than when they're alone, especially when Mom or Dad adjusts the play to the child's level.

Brothers and sisters make even better playmates, since they usually enjoy the play more than adults do. Toddlers love to imitate other children and can learn a lot from them, especially in the realm of practical skills. (You may have heard of a neighbor's one-year-old who toilet-trained himself early by imitating his older siblings.) This ability to learn from other children is one of a number of reasons it is a good idea to begin arranging play dates for your child in the second year. An early-childhood music or dance program, which combines stimulating rhythmic games and melodies with child-to-child and parent-child interaction, might be a fun activity for you both. But don't forget to let your one-year-old play on his own as well. He needs to learn to entertain himself to some degree, to enjoy his own company and have the satisfaction of discovering things for himself.

THE TOY BOX
At Fourteen Months

It's Saturday, and Josh is enjoying a deliciously unstructured morning hanging around the house with Mom and Dad. Dad has been helping him stack some blocks. Josh can make a stack of two, but Dad can add even more blocks on top of that. He picks up a cylinder. "Look, Josh. Those blocks are square, but I can put a round one on top," Dad says, and he demonstrates.

Suddenly Josh feels tired of blocks. He toddles off, heading by habit toward the toy basket. Ah! There's his duck—the plastic one that squeaks when he squeezes or punches it. He grabs it and smacks it on the edge of the basket, listening for the squeak.

"Oh, you found your yellow duck," Dad says, going over to him. He knows better than to insist on continuing with the blocks. "Look." He points to one of the duck's eyes and traces it with his finger. "The duck's eye is round, like the round block. It makes a circle shape."

Josh looks from the toy to his dad and back again. "Wownd." He's heard the word before but didn't know what it meant. He still doesn't—but he knows it has something to do with both the block and the eye.

"And look," Dad continues. "That button on your overalls is round, too. Daddy's buttons are round. There are lots of round things in this house."

Josh listens intently. He likes Dad's happy tone of voice. He also likes the connections Dad is making among different objects in his world. He drops the plastic duck. "Wownd!" he says, and giggles as it squeaks.

HOW HARD SHOULD YOU PUSH?: PACING YOUR CHILD'S PLAY

Sometimes at the playground I've heard parents suggest that the kind of directed play I've described might place an unnecessary burden on their children. They watch other parents asking their very young toddlers questions, nudging them on toward more experimentation, providing new words for their vocabulary, and they wonder whether this kind of "pushing" is just a reflection of the parents' ambition and not in the best interest of the child. They prefer to let their children move along at their own pace, they say. Childhood is short enough without parents pushing babies to do better from the very beginning.

Of course, pressuring a one-year-old to achieve for his parents can get out of hand. No one advocates "drilling" an eighteen-month-old, insisting that he perform a new skill in order to receive a reward, and so on. But the fact is that while parental coaching doesn't have much effect on how quickly a baby acquires motor skills such as crawling or walking, stimulating play inspired by the child's existing interests does literally encourage brain development. It is not necessary to pressure a child to "make him smarter"—young children love to learn! It is his caregivers' job to offer him the *opportunity* to learn more about what interests him whenever possible, in the context of a loving, supportive environment. Just as Andrew and Cass's mom pointed out in "A Parent's Story" earlier in this chapter, letting your child know you're available and following his lead is the best way to expand his understanding of his world.

Whether your child picks up new skills more or less quickly than your co-worker's child, both one-year-olds will learn them in roughly the same sequence. Children with Down's syndrome and other developmental conditions follow the same blueprint toward maturity, though not with the same speed or richness as children who are spared those challenges. In most cases there is no need to worry if your child is not yet putting things into containers at fifteen months. He's probably just not interested in filling things up right now. Keep in mind also that, as we saw in the previous chapter, the second year is filled to the brim with physical challenges; during periods when your little one is obsessed with learning to walk or develop certain fine-motor skills, he will probably spend less time playing with non-movement-related toys and games.

It is a fact, too, as Dr. Howard Gardner pointed out in his groundbreaking book *Frames of Mind,* that we humans display a wide variety of types of intelligence. Your child may be a genius at discerning emotions but not particularly advanced in his ability to categorize shapes. He may "specialize" in musical ability but possess a less than dazzling visual sense. Many of these abilities will develop only with time, and your child's performance in any one area will probably rise and fall as the years progress. It makes sense, then, to enjoy and encourage whatever skills manifest themselves and not to worry too much about his "slower" areas.

In the end, the most important lesson for your child to learn at this age is that he is well loved and that his world is a reasonably predictable place, nevertheless full of delightful surprises. The wisest parents are those who think for a bit about the ways in which they can enrich their child's experience and then, after implementing those ideas, devote themselves to having fun. Remember, whatever your toddler's intellectual level turns out to be, it can only be enhanced through time spent interacting with you.

Playing with Your Child

Playing with a young child doesn't always come naturally. In most cases, doing it well takes a little focus and practice, and maybe even letting go of some grown-up expectations. In general, your one-year-old will play most happily when his entire body is involved. His brain is literally not capable of taking in much information "symbolically," through abstract concepts or talk (though, in my estimation, educational computer games are moving even one-year-olds toward such concepts sooner). This is why nursery songs and children's chants are such a delight for a child— they provide new information through his senses in the form of pleasing rhythms and sounds, movement (such as hand-clapping), and direct interaction with other people.

When playing, make sure to get down on the floor with him as often as possible, playing "at his level" rather than talking down to him. Listen to what he says about what he's doing, and respond by taking the play one step further in an interesting direction. Make eye contact. Avoid distracting stimuli, like a television going in the background. Give him plenty of positive reinforcement, and he will come to view play—and learning—as one of life's greatest pleasures.

BOOKS:
TOYS THAT TALK

Parents sometimes become so conditioned to playing actively with their infants that they forget to initiate book-reading until late in the second year, or they read books only at bedtime. This is a shame, not only because storytime can be used very effectively in establishing daily routines and

This pair enjoys the experience of reading together, even though they're not on the "same page."

encouraging language development (as we will see in later chapters), but because books are literally "toys that talk," and they provide the perfect opportunity for the two of you to engage in some stimulating play. Pulling your one-year-old onto your lap for a story sets up just the kind of loving, focused interaction your child loves best. The feel of the book, the challenge of turning its pages, the brightly colored story illustrations, the coziness of sitting close to you, and the sound of your voice reading all pleasantly engage the senses. Meanwhile, each new page brings a host of concepts and images for a curious one-year-old to ponder. Your involvement—naming objects in the pictures for him, asking him questions now and then, and comparing bits of the story to people, animals, or situations he already knows—keeps his neurons firing and his brain working hard.

As with other aspects of parent-child play, even when your little one doesn't seem to be paying attention—even when his gaze wanders or he flips through the pages, skipping half the story in the process—he is learning something. So be patient. Don't worry about the storyline so much right now, and don't insist on reading to the end. Just focus on introducing the pleasures of storytime to your child, not only at bedtime but often throughout the day, and use it to demonstrate once again how loved he truly is.

IF YOU'RE CONCERNED
Developmental Delays

As I have pointed out before, performance checklists for toddlers are often inaccurate when applied to a specific child, but they do give a very general idea of the steps your child must take to achieve cognitive maturity. If he is less than two months behind the chart in achieving a certain skill, there is probably nothing to worry about. However, again, your own instincts are the most reliable diagnostic tool. If your one-year-old does seem to be falling behind cognitively—if he is not mastering skills at all as opposed to accomplishing them slowly—or if he appears listless, unfocused, or uninterested in exploring his world, he might have a hearing, vision, or other problem. Increasingly, children's hearing is tested at birth—a good thing, since a lot can be done to correct such problems if they are diagnosed early. But if your child's hearing and vision haven't yet been tested, it's certainly not too late to discuss your concerns with your pediatrician and perhaps set up an evaluation. The sooner your child receives the help he needs, the sooner he can resume his place on the road to greater understanding.

SEE YOU LATER, MOMMY!

Nearly a year has passed, and it's almost time for Craig's second birthday party, an event that Leah hopes will be as much fun and as memorable as the first one. Feeling a little nostalgic, she pops the videotape of his first birthday into the VCR while twenty-three-month-old Craig busies himself with his toy box nearby. Suddenly there on the screen is Craig at twelve months, staring in wide-eyed wonder as a bubble drifts past his face. Leah giggles, watching his expression as, on the TV screen, she gets up and goes inside the house.

How different he is now, Leah thinks as she looks from the teary one-year-old on the screen to the busy two-year-old at the toy box and back again. *His understanding of how the world works has progressed by light-years. Now when I blow bubbles, he watches them pop, then orders me to make some more—that is, when he doesn't insist on blowing the bubbles himself. His understanding of what happens to me when I'm gone has changed completely, too. Now when I leave him at the child-care center, most days he waves good-bye and tells me, "Mommy go work!" He still cries once in a while when I drop him off or even pick him up, but I think he knows now that I'll always be back at the end of the day. All that talk and repetition has paid off, I guess.*

Leah nestles deeper into the sofa cushions, watching her televised self rush back to reassure her crying one-year-old that she's still there—she just stepped out of sight for a while. She glances over at her two-year-old son. "Where my car?" he says without looking at her, poking around in his toy box. "Help, Mommy." And a moment later, "Oh. I got!"

He holds up the car and gives her a big smile. He did it! Leah grins as she watches him cross the room with his prize. He knew that his toy was somewhere around here, and he found it. He solved the problem himself. What an independent little boy.

Common Cognitive Achievements in the Second Year

12 MONTHS   Turns pages of a book

Puts objects in a container

Can sometimes stack two cubes

Uses toy telephone like a real telephone

15 MONTHS   Likes to scribble

Builds tower of two or three blocks

Closes container

Names one picture

Points to two pictures

Becomes interested in cause and effect

Practices new tasks over and over

18 MONTHS   Can tell the difference between circles and squares

Can point to doll's body parts

Names three objects

Identifies objects in a photograph

Follows simple directions

Memory improves

21 MONTHS   Can tell difference between circles, squares, and triangles

Shows greater accuracy with shape box

Attends to story longer

Matches shoes with correct family member

Is beginning to understand concept of "now"

24 MONTHS Builds tower of blocks, train of blocks

Engages in fantasy play

Begins to plan behaviors

Engages in creative problem-solving

Begins to understand concept of "soon" or "after lunch" (but not "next week" or "at four o'clock")

FIRST-PERSON SINGULAR

Now record your observations of your own child's neurological development. What are his all-consuming obsessions as the months pass? How has his play evolved? When did you first see that he had planned an action ahead of time? Has he started to play imaginary games with his dolls or action figures? Keeping in mind the variety of kinds of intelligence, make a note of any evidence you see of the emergence of musical, visual, interpersonal, or other non-mainstream skills or interests. As his neurological and verbal abilities develop side by side, you will see a merging of intelligences that leads your child to a new level of thinking. He will let you know through his words what steps he's made. Write down those funny little sentences before you forget. You'll enjoy recalling them in the years to come!

READER'S NOTES

_____

_____

_____

_____

_____

_____

_____

_____

_____

_____

_____

_____

_____

_____

_____

_____

_____

_____

CHAPTER 4

Listen to Me!—My Verbal Abilities

etween twelve and twenty-four months, your child is likely to progress from understanding (but not yet saying) a dozen words to knowing two hundred or more.

Sharon's firstborn, Dana, was just over a year old when Sharon discovered that she was pregnant again. Initially, Sharon was delighted at the idea of having two children so close in age. But as the pregnancy continued and became increasingly difficult (Sharon was confined to bed for the last couple of months), she felt guilty about how often Dana's needs had to take a backseat to the developing baby's. Sharon became particularly concerned when she realized, after baby Jacob's birth, that twenty-one-month-old Dana was hardly speaking yet. Checking the standard parenting books, Sharon was horrified to see that according to the lists of developmental milestones Dana should know more than a hundred words by now and be able to say a few dozen. It seemed to Sharon that Dana hardly ever said more than "Mommy," "dog," and a few other nouns! Worried that she had not spent enough time with her daughter (who had gone to stay with her grandparents several times during the pregnancy), Sharon began reading to her several times each day. When she pointed to a picture and asked Dana what it was, both mother and daughter became increasingly frustrated by Dana's inability to say the word. Soon the reading sessions became so unpleasant that Sharon feared they might be working against Dana's speaking ability rather than encouraging it.

Sharon's situation is not unusual. In my clinical experience, I've seen how difficult it is not to worry when a child's verbal development seems to lag behind that of others the same age. Concerns about how a non-speaking child's relative silence relates to her intelligence, anxiety over whether a recent life change or other difficulty might have slowed her progress, and guilty thoughts about how we might have stimulated more verbal development if only we'd known—all of these get in the way of observing the child objectively to see whether there really is a problem. In fact, though, children's verbal development varies widely and can stop and start for a number of reasons. What we had assumed would be a steady progression of nonsense sounds to single words to two-word sentences to fluent speech is instead a journey full of leaps and regressions, often influenced by the child's passing emotional or physical state. More important than the *number* of words your child can say is whether she frequently gets frustrated because she can't think of the word she wants, whether she can say more words now than she could a month ago, whether she understands a good deal of what you say to her, and whether her hearing is satisfactory. Certainly, such events as a difficult pregnancy, a change in caregivers, or a move to a new house are likely to slow or even temporarily stop a child's progress in speaking. If her development does not pick up again after a couple of weeks and you truly feel there's cause for concern, it wouldn't hurt to check with her pediatrician. But in most cases, children catch up verbally within a year or so. Meanwhile, if you actually count the words she says (in her own way) over the course of a few days, you may be surprised at how many she already knows.

In this chapter, we will examine the ways in which your child's verbal abilities have been developing since before she was born. We will see how quickly she learned to distinguish her parents' language from foreign tongues and how she picked up the rhythms and characteristic sounds of your language before she learned to speak actual words. We'll follow her development as she learns first to understand words, then to say some of them. We'll see how gestures and facial expressions often precede language, and the funny ways in which she may confuse words and their meanings at first. The basis of all her learning in the area of communication is, first, listening to your speech and then imitating you. We will explore the importance of talking a great deal to your child in order to stimulate her own speech development. Finally, we will discuss adults' regrettable tendency to confuse a one-year-old's verbal ability with overall intelligence. Many other issues and concerns—such as a new baby in the house or an individual child's simple tendency to think things through privately—can get in the way of a toddler's desire to talk out loud. Between the ages of twelve and twenty-four months, your child's ability to communicate should be measured not by how many words she can say at any given time but by how content she seems to be with her own progress.

"BA-BA!": VERBAL ACHIEVEMENTS BEFORE AGE ONE

If you've ever tried to learn a foreign language, you have to be impressed by your one-year-old's comparative ease in picking up yours—particularly since she learns most of what she knows from the natural context of conversation, not from specific lessons aimed at systematically increasing her knowledge. Many parents have decided that their child must simply be a genius because of her ability to internalize and use a language at such a phenomenal rate. In fact, though, language acquisition is an instinct, like learning to walk, and all normal babies' brains are superwired for the task. Your one-year-old finds it easier to learn English than you ever found it to learn French because, from birth to age three, she is experiencing one of those neurological "critical periods" for language. Her ability to acquire her mother tongue (or any other language) will never be as primed as it is right now.

Recent studies by Dr. Patricia Kuhl of the University of Washington and others have shown that very young infants can already recognize the sounds of their mother tongue, responding differently when they hear a foreign language spoken. By approximately seven months of age, they have grown sufficiently familiar with their language's typical rhythms and sounds to begin separating distinct words from the stream of ordinary conversation. This ability to hear distinct words leads very quickly to the nine-month-old's first wordlike vocalizations. At this age, she begins limiting her babbling to sounds that "make sense" in terms of phonemes, or sound combinations, in her native language (though they don't actually mean anything). The daughter of an English speaker, for example, will say "Ga-ga," but probably not "Gda-gda." A Polish baby, on the other hand, is very likely to practice the latter sound. At around this age, your baby probably also began to understand and respond to some words and expressions, such as "Do you want your teddy bear?" and "Wave bye-bye!"

Toward the end of the first year, babies begin *jargoning*—that is, babbling in a way that sounds like your language (it has the same rhythms and sounds) but still isn't actual words. Sometimes jargoning seems to be an actual language itself, since a child this age may regularly use a certain word ("da," for example) to denote a specific object (such as a teddy bear). Later, her approximation of the real word will grow more accurate ("beh" for bear), and the original term transferred to an object whose name sounds more like it ("da" will come to mean "Daddy"). All of these developments set the stage for the language burst that takes place in the second year.

EASING THE WAY
Word Games

Moving into her second year, your child continues to benefit from focused attention as you converse. As she watches and listens to you speak, she is taking in not only your words but your inflection, pitch, and speech rhythms as well. Playing with your words—varying each of the qualities listed above—will make learning language into a pleasant experience while it "tunes up her ears" for better expression. Here are some specific "talking games" for parents and toddlers from "Read*Write*Now*," a wonderful guide for parents available on-line at www.ed.gov.

All parents enjoy trying to teach their one-year-olds to sing the ABCs. Next time, try singing the song to your little one in a variety of funny variations—pausing dramatically between phrases; singing it in a high, peeping voice like a bird; and then singing the song in a deep, dark voice like a bear. Let your child try to mimic you if she likes. By playing this game, you will not only familiarize her with letters but expand your own range of expression.

You can help your child increase her vocabulary by reading to her often. When reading one of her favorite stories, use your voice to draw attention to a special, new word. Say the word in a funny way, sing it, say it loud or soft, and make funny faces when you say it. For the rest of the day, show your child different ways the word can be used. The next time you read together, choose a new word.

If your child hasn't yet started saying her own name, play this game: Ask her, "What's your name?" If she answers correctly, say, "Yes, that's your name. Your name is [Dana]." If she doesn't say her name, you say, "Your name is [Dana]. What's your name?" and repeat again until she says her name correctly. Once she knows her name, you can have fun with it. Look at your child. "What did you say your name was? [Dana]? I thought your name was Snicklefritz." Of course, you can also play with your own and other loved ones' names, as in "My name is Mother Goose. Is that my name?"

Ways to encourage speech at any time include using short sentences, speaking slowly, talking in a higher register than usual, and demonstrating your love of communicating by varying your inflection and saying new words or phrases with careful attention and enthusiasm. (Speak and read aloud to your child a bit more dramatically than you might to an adult.) Just as important in encouraging speech is learning to listen to your child and responding appropriately to what she's trying to tell you. By echoing her inner experience with your own verbal response (watching her eat her favorite food and remarking, "Dana *loves* broccoli!"), you will demonstrate to her the power of words to create a bond of understanding between human beings.

"MORE COOKIE!":
VERBAL ACHIEVEMENTS FROM
ONE TO TWO

Between the ages of twelve and twenty-four months, your child is likely to progress from understanding (but not yet saying) perhaps a dozen words to knowing two hundred or more. How many of these words she actually *says* is not the critical issue at this age—although the fact that words, unlike other developmental progressions, are easy to count often results in comparisons with other children. Some one-year-olds are quite happy comprehending speech without feeling a need to talk back. In any case, there will be some kind of progression from her more sophisticated comprehension ability toward better speaking skills. However many words she can say by her second birthday, the number will certainly be more than she could say on her first.

Receptive speech is the term for the kind of communication your child has probably already begun to learn by the time she turns one. This means that if you ask her to get her "blankie" out of the laundry basket, she'll show you that she understands by either getting the blanket or by shaking her head no. She has begun to understand, if not always to name, a number of people and objects as well—usually those most meaningful to her such as "Mama," "Dada," "blankie," and "dog."

Twelve months can be a funny period for language, because your child is likely to spend quite a bit of time "pretending" to hold conversations, declaiming away like a seasoned orator, her inflections and rhythms stunningly accurate but her words for the most part nonsensical. This is one instance when you will be bowled over by what brilliant mimics children are—she will sound *exactly* like your mother or her brother without actually saying one English word! Still, only her family and caregivers are likely to know what she means.

The word "no" may become an object of endless fascination at around this time. As she says "No!" to this and "No!" to that, you may wonder whether your generally cheerful twelve-month-old is hitting the "terrible two's" alarmingly early. In fact, though, she's just reveling in the power of this easy-to-say word and watching, fascinated, for listeners' reactions. Chances are that "No!" will take up quite a long residence in your household from now on. Its inherent power can be irresistible to very small children, who must sometimes feel it's all the power they've got.

In most cases, the first half of the second year is a bit slow in terms of verbal ability. This is partly because your child is so focused on learning to walk and develop other motor skills that there's little energy left to focus on language. You may wonder at times whether she's making any progress, as she seems content to use her handful of nouns and just point and grunt for anything else she wants. Never fear, at around eighteen months, having mastered her ability to walk, she will likely begin spewing forth an absolute explosion of words. According to many scientifically documented child-development scales, children acquire on average half a dozen or more words per day between age eighteen months and six years. This is truly amazing when you think about it. Her word use will also become more reliable—you won't have to figure out what a sound means quite as often. She will begin at eighteen months with a vocabulary of anywhere from three to fifty words and an ability to say short sentences of two or three words ("More milk," "Dana go home," etc.), and end up at age two telling you quite clearly what she wants or needs with words.

THE TOY BOX
At Fifteen Months

Anne is mopping the living-room floor, so she has parked fifteen-month-old Petra on the other side of the baby gate dividing the living and dining rooms. Petra stands at the gate frowning, as Mommy moves back and forth, back and forth, with the mop. "Tull!" she says, raising an imperious arm and pointing at the toy box at the opposite end of the living room. Anne looks up at her. "Turtle?" she asks. She walks over to the toy box and pulls out a stuffed turtle. "Is this what you want?"

"No!" Petra says with great relish, a grin playing around her mouth. She points again. "Petra, tull!"

Perplexed, Anne holds up a teddy bear. "Tull?" she asks, trying not to feel silly.

"No!" Petra says with even greater relish.

Anne suspects that this entire exercise is taking place just so

Petra has the excuse to say "No!" Still, she pulls out the well-worn toy phone. "Telephone?" she asks tentatively.

"No! Tull!"

Suddenly Anne experiences a moment of blazing insight. "Tull" means "pull"! Petra wants the caterpillar pull-toy her grandfather bought her last week. She's been obsessed with it ever since, pulling it everywhere as she works on her walking skills.

"I know," Anne says, smiling at Petra. She gets out the pull-toy and holds it up. "*Pull* the caterpillar, right?"

"Tull!" Petra is probably thinking, *Finally, Mom.* She stretches her arm over the baby gate. She *must* get that pull-toy now. Better word skills can wait their turn. Right now she needs to walk and pull.

"THAT'S WHAT I SAID": HOW LANGUAGE DEVELOPS

We tend to think of our children's language development as something they accomplish pretty much on their own. But, of course, when you think about it, learning to communicate verbally is impossible without people to communicate *with.* Your one-year-old's speech skills are the result of a joint effort between herself and those around her. When she first tries to "speak" to you by repeating sounds you don't recognize as words, you nevertheless naturally make an effort to imagine what the sound might mean. When *you* speak to *her,* she goes through the same process. It is this focus on each other's efforts to communicate—the guessing at meaning, the questioning repetition, and the mirroring back of comprehension or puzzlement at the sound of a word—that lays the groundwork for speech.

If you have ever visited a foreign country where you had a very limited command of the language, you probably remember what a bewildering cacophony of sound seemed to envelop you everywhere you went. Think back to how you managed to get the things you needed while you were there. Probably you just pointed at objects, such as items at a market, nodded a lot, and tried to say their names. If you heard a word (such as

More and more, your toddler's pointing gestures will be accompanied by actual words.

"*grazie*" or "*playa*") often enough, you would probably start to use it yourself once in a while and feel pretty good about your ability to participate in all the "noise" surrounding you.

Your child deals with her world in much the same way. Just like you in a foreign land, she points at things and tries to name them. At around twelve months, her initial vocabulary consists of words that mean a lot to her: the names of people around her, her favorite objects, and things that fascinate because they move or make interesting noises (such as "cat" or "car"). Soon she will announce the names of foods she eats, articles of her clothing, and the names of people outside her immediate circle. At first, her parents (or even a sibling) may be the only ones who understand what she's trying to say. To these loved ones, "ba" means "bottle," *obviously.* Parents' tendency to repeat the word their baby says, their faces lighting up with pride, helps refine the child's pronunciation while reinforcing her desire to keep talking. Through this "name, echo, name" process, the one-year-old's utterance will gradually come to sound more and more like the actual word—though often a child is three years old before just about everyone can understand her.

Clearly, even learning the names of objects is not an easy task, and it's something of a miracle how easily babies manage to get it done. Just think about how perplexed you might be in that hypothetical foreign country if the person standing next to you pointed at a bird in the sky and said, "Yah!" What does "yah" mean? you'd wonder. Does it refer to the bird, to an aspect of the bird (its long wings or its blue color), to the act of flying, or to how high it is in the sky? As research by Dr. Ellen Markman, author of *Categorization and Naming in Children,* and others has shown, babies solve this initial problem by assuming that a naming word (such as "juice") refers to a whole entity (the juice) rather than to just one aspect of it (the color). Once they know the word "juice," they can go on to learn the subsidiary words, such as "sweet," "orange," and so on. This system doesn't always work. A one-year-old might *over*generalize, calling cups of water, milk, and soda "juice," too. (They all come in a cup, don't they?) They can also *under*generalize, calling only the drink in their own cup "juice."

Of course, these sources of confusion straighten themselves out over the months as children's brains develop, thanks to feedback from you and with more observation on their part. By eighteen months, language skills have often progressed to the point at which your child can start ordering you around with a technique called *telegraphic speech,* so called because it's as simple and urgent as a telegram. If your child is this age already, you are no doubt well accustomed to hearing "Mommy come" and "Daddy go" and "Get ball" around the house. Even telegraphic speech can be confusing to parents, though. What does "truck me" mean, for example? Does the child want the truck? Is she saying that it's her truck? Does she mean the truck is small like her? Trying to guess the message in those two little words can get pretty funny at times. It helps, parents historically have found, to pay attention to the child's gestures and other nonverbal communication as well. But even then, expect quite a few misunderstandings at both ends of the conversation during this year.

Dr. Steven Pinker, author of *The Language Instinct: How the Mind Creates Language,* and other experts point out that no matter what culture your child belongs to, the steps she takes in language development remain more or less the same. Babies name objects before moving on to verbs, no matter what language they use to say those first words. They generalize in the same way, assuming that a word refers to an entire object rather than a part of it. And they make the same mistakes as they begin learning how to construct their sentences.

A BABY'S-EYE VIEW
Look Over There!

Sun, fifteen-month-old Irene thinks as she and her mom go out for a walk in the neighborhood. She sees something move on the sidewalk ahead. A word pops out: "Dog!" "Yes, dog!" her mother repeats, giving her hand a squeeze. "Big dog, right, Irene?"

But Irene's attention has already wandered. As the two of them stop at an intersection, Irene watches the traffic light change and a truck drive off. She pulls on her mother's hand and points at it. "Tuck!"

"What's that, sweetie?" her mother responds. "Oh, yes. The truck goes! The light turns green and it goes."

Irene feels a physical tingle at the sound of Mommy's words.

She has seen cars go but hasn't had the word to describe what she sees. Mommy has used that word before. But now the sound of it has connected with a meaning for the first time. "Go," she says experimentally, looking off toward the disappearing truck. "Tuck go!"

Her mother looks down at her. She gives her a big smile and squeezes her hand again. "Yes, Irene. The truck goes!" she says.

Irene smiles, too, as mother and daughter start to cross the street. "Tuck go." She feels the sound of the words in her mouth. She sees another dog. Maybe dogs go, too . . .

LISTEN TO ME: FROM IMITATING TO EXPRESSING THROUGH WORDS

By eighteen months of age, your child will have become quite an accomplished mimic, in both her behavior and her words. If you have a tendency to say "Awesome" or some other somewhat unusual word or phrase when in her presence, expect to hear it back from her very soon. She may not use it appropriately, but she will almost certainly get the inflection and facial expressions exactly right. As she practices her speech, she will not only talk to other people, but will often talk to herself. Just as she babbled happily to herself in her crib in the morning when she was younger, so she will chatter away to no one as she plays with her toys, walks around, etc. Often she narrates her activities as they happen. Some theorists believe that children do this not just to play with words but to make sense out of their day, re-creating their experience through language. This is a truly sophisticated accomplishment, involving the use of mental symbols and abstract thought, and it is fascinating to watch.

By around twenty-one months, many children move from the apparent self-involvement of narrating their actions to themselves to the more spontaneous conversation of the two-year-old. At this point, your child may initiate much more of the conversation than before. She will be more likely to notice if you aren't really interested in what she's saying or if you are distracted. She'll increasingly respond to the tone of your voice more than just the words (stopping what she's doing when she hears a sharp-toned "Sweetie," for example).

By this time, "Mine!" has probably long been a popular staple of her verbal repertoire. But she may now become interested in who owns the other objects in her world. "Mommy comb!" she may tell her father, outraged, when he starts to borrow his wife's comb one morning. And she will happily wander the house calling, "Where Daddy keys?"

Q & A
Simon Says

Q: My eighteen-month-old has suddenly begun spouting a number of "inappropriate" words at the worst possible times. She shouts "s—t" whenever she falls down or stubs her toe. The other day my mother-in-law was visiting when my daughter cruised through the room yelling, "Where damn phone?" What's a parent to do?

A: It's a fact of life that one-year-olds are incurable mimics. In general, if a word gets said in your house, you can bet your child will be saying it herself soon—particularly when the word is invoked with the level of emotion with which most people use curse words. Your angry or embarrassed "Don't say that!" will only make the word more fascinating, an irresistible temptation at this age.

If you are uncomfortable with the idea of your sweet-faced child's cursing like the proverbial sailor, either at home or in public, your only recourse is to avoid using those words yourself. You will have to do this long before she is able to repeat them. Children often understand and "learn" words far earlier than they begin to speak them. If, as in your case, your child has already begun using such words, your best bet is to gently and nonchalantly give her alternatives. Next time you stub your toe, say "sugar" instead, loud enough for her to hear.

LET'S TALK:
THE RHYTHMS OF CONVERSATION

Watching your child learn the meaning of word after word is a joyful experience, but verbal communication consists of more than just the formation of words and letters, more than just putting sounds together. Your child naturally understands that she must not only expand her vocabulary and learn the basic rules of grammar and semantics but also pick up the art of when to pause in conversation, when to talk, comprehend why it's useless for both people to talk at the same time, and so on. You have heard her practice with the rhythms of speech since she began to babble. Now she must work on how and when to modulate the volume of her voice (reminding her to use her soft "inside voice" or louder "outside voice" can be helpful) and on the meaning and value of eye contact.

This is not an easy set of rules to learn, so be patient if your child stutters at times in her eagerness to get her idea across to you or looks away sometimes while you're talking. Don't rush her. Let her work out what she needs to say in her own good time. Then respond naturally, clearly, and with enthusiasm. Keep in mind that stammering is quite common at this age—it's just a sign of temporary overload, a momentary inability to keep pace with what is happening in her brain. Refusing to run roughshod over her during these awkward moments will give her the chance to practice her verbal skills and increase her confidence in her ability to communicate.

By the time she reaches her second birthday, your child will probably have mastered many of the social, speaking, and listening skills it takes to carry on a successful conversation. She will have had experience in taking turns, recognizing her own turn to talk, and knowing when the person to whom she's speaking doesn't understand what she's said. She will know the signs of attention and willingness to continue talking— eye contact, body posture, and so on. (I've seen two-year-olds in the hospital waiting room, for example, notice that their parents have stopped listening to them while they're filling out paperwork. The children literally turn their parents' heads toward them with their hands to get their attention, then blithely continue talking.) Your two-year-old will still be more likely to converse with adults than with other children, but that will change remarkably soon. In just a few months more, you will see her carrying on earnest tête-à-têtes with her equally verbal peers.

A PARENT'S STORY
Pillow Talk

"From the time Bobby was about eight months old, he loved to babble to himself at bedtime," his mother, Elise, told me. "He was quite a talker. I used to laugh, hearing him in his crib chatting to the walls. After he started talking, I'd hear him in bed at night muttering about his day. He'd talk about what he'd had for lunch and what he'd done with his sitter and how he'd made birthday cakes out of sand at the playground that afternoon. Starting when he was about eighteen months old, I got into the habit of passing by his door every once in a while to hear what new words he was using or find out what events of the day he was reviewing. I was often surprised by what he'd focused on or seemed to be processing. It helped me figure out where his interests were at that particular time, so I could expand on them the next day. Listening to him at bedtime is also how I found out that he was picking up some Spanish words from my husband, who's from Puerto Rico. My husband usually speaks English to Bobby. I didn't even know he'd heard Spanish!

SMART TALK:
HOW LANGUAGE REFLECTS
COGNITIVE ADVANCES

Because language takes its big leap forward at the same time as several other cognitive skills—that is, at about eighteen months—its appearance is generally considered a sign of the progress infants and toddlers make on their way to early childhood. Your child's increased verbal ability does not *cause* the other cognitive leaps of this period (the idea that she can make things happen, the concept of the "self" versus "other," etc.), but it is a *signal* that a number of separate skills have begun coming together to make a greater whole, a consequence of the brain development described in the previous chapter. Basically, increased verbal sophistication signals the one-year-old's ability to think symbolically—to begin to play out past, present, or future events on the stage of the mind.

What language does do is radically restructure your child's world, mainly by dividing it into nonverbal and verbal experience and introducing a new and more refined sense of categories. It introduces a sense of the passage of time—of past, present, and future events. And it frames experiences in words that can be retained as conscious memories—separate from the preverbal, but extremely important—daily accumulation of unconscious impressions such as "Mom loves me" or "Mom doesn't love me." This new ability to "log" thoughts and experiences and re-create them in her mind allows your child to ponder and respond to a much wider variety of data and leads to even greater and more varied cognitive growth.

IF YOU'RE CONCERNED
Verbal Delays

As with all aspects of development at this age, a very broad spectrum exists regarding the language development of perfectly "normal" children. If your twenty-month-old seems to prefer looking at picture books rather than engaging in conversation all the time, she's probably perfectly fine. Keep in mind that she may be currently focusing on another area of development or that she simply isn't particularly extroverted by nature.

It's also vital to remember that all children this age understand much more language than they can speak. If your child has older siblings, she may not feel the need to say much, since others are speaking for her. (The same is true if you provide her with all her needs before she has to ask for them.) Children in bilingual homes also tend to spend some time sorting out the different sounds before beginning to speak either language. (This is not a cause for alarm; such a child is usually back on track by the time she enters school.) Generally, if your child listens to you, responds to your questions or directions ("Where is your juice?"), and otherwise demonstrates that she understands your words (pointing to an object you name), you can be sure that her "window of oppor-tunity" for language is being put to good use.

If you have explored all these possibilities, however, and con-tinue to feel that your child may be speech-delayed, consider whether she might have a hearing problem. (She should have had her hearing tested by her pediatrician, but if she hasn't, make sure it is tested now.) If her hearing is normal, she could conceivably have a speech or learning disorder that should be diagnosed by a professional. By age two, most significant problems can be either accurately identified or ruled out by a speech pathologist or other specialist.

HOW SMART IS SHE?: VERBAL SKILLS AND GENERAL INTELLIGENCE

Because we place so much importance on the ability to communicate through words, it's not surprising that any hesitation in the process of learning to talk often has parents panicking over their child's intelligence level. As I've said, it is crucial to keep in mind that there is truly an enormous range in the rate of language acquisition during this year.

I know from personal experience how hard it is to separate the con-cepts of verbal performance and intelligence, as well as the ideas of verbal *ability* and verbal *performance.* My own son, Alex, appeared to be speech-delayed when he was two years old, and I was the only one who wasn't worried. Alex didn't seem frustrated by his limited range of speech, and he and his twin brother, Matthew, were communicating just fine. How-ever, my friends and relatives continued to point out to me that Matthew was comparatively advanced in his verbal skills, so surely Alex's relative silence was a source of concern. Finally—partly through peer pressure and partly through guilt (what kind of a mother was I not to worry?)—I did start to doubt my own gut feeling that Alex was okay, and I made an appointment for him at the hospital where I work.

The hospital staff tested Alex's hearing first. They played a tape of a cow mooing. Alex easily tracked where the sound was coming from and handled the other tasks well, so his hearing was fine. Next, Alex's expressive speech was tested through a speech and language evaluation. In the end, the verdict was "He obviously understands us. He has several words and lots of the right signs are there. He's just not ready to talk much yet."

In fact, Alex's verbal development started to kick in less than six months later. Now he talks much more than his twin brother. But he continues to be the very thoughtful boy he always was, pondering a new situation first, then talking his way through the activity.

The moral of the story is that I could have trusted my intuition in this situation, since it was based on what I knew about him, but having a trained professional check his hearing turned out to be a big relief. Language skills are such a loaded issue for us, connected as they are to how we think the child will do in the world, that it's probably better just to quell all the fears we can.

One fact to consider is that, in general, girls talk sooner and more fluently than boys. Even at twenty-one months, many boys may still speak chiefly in one- or, at most, two-word sentences. Many may still be using jargon. Others will communicate chiefly through pointing, gesturing, and grunting. A twenty-one-month-old girl, by contrast, might already be speaking in short sentences, though still with a "babyish" pronunciation that's often difficult to understand.

Language, like other areas of development, proceeds at its own pace. It does not make sense to jump to the conclusion that a one-year-old who is slow to begin talking has a cognitive delay. If the cause isn't her current focus on motor skills or the fact that she has a new baby brother at home, she may simply be in an environment in which the adults don't talk to her a great deal. (Though there is no evidence that specifically trying to teach a child to talk speeds up the *rate* at which she learns, it is known that the wider the variety of language experiences she has, the more enriched her vocabulary will become.) Or she may simply have a quiet nature.

As I pointed out earlier, even most two-year-olds stammer and stutter at times. Their speech is coming in so rapidly at that age that it's just very difficult to keep up with it. Talking at this age must feel to a child sometimes like falling over her feet while learning to walk. Again, it's important to help her along during this phase without always saying the words for her. Try to stay attuned to when your child wants your help expressing her thoughts (maybe when she's tired) or when she'd prefer to struggle along on her own. In general, it's best not to voice her thoughts before she's tried to do so herself, but if it's clear she's about to lose it, try asking a leading question that provides her with some of the words she needs. (If it's obvious that she's hungry, for example, ask, "Do you want cereal or a banana?" instead of "What do you want?") Trying to express oneself at this age, when there's so very much to say, can be quite frustrating. Your efforts to help her ease the frustration will probably be met with gratitude, if you don't crowd in too close.

Without question, the leaps your child will make in language acquisition between twelve and twenty-four months will amaze and delight you. Just keep in mind the broad range that exists in the rate of this development, and resist the urge to compare your child's progress to another's. Remember also that learning to talk is not a steady process. As Dr. T. Berry Brazelton points out, there will probably be periods of regression when your chatty two-year-old reverts to the speech patterns of her younger self. (This frequently occurs after the appearance of a new baby or a new caregiver, for example.) There are also bound to be breakdowns in communication once in a while, leading to frustration on both sides. Clearly, the frustration is worth the reward, however. By the time she's two, your child's world has grown dramatically, embracing both her sensory experience and whatever information she takes in through language. It's a fact—as you might make a point of telling your little one—that her exciting steps forward in learning to talk mean she's truly "a big girl" now.

Q & A

What Did You Say?

Q: Our fifteen-month-old daughter, Melissa, has been talking up a storm since before her first birthday. She talks to her stuffed animals when she wakes up in the morning, to us all day, to the mailman, to her older brothers and all their friends, to the trees, to herself, and to anyone else who happens by. The problem is, no one can understand more than a word or two of what she says! Even those of us in her family who have listened to her talk for months now have to ask her to repeat herself over and over again, and most of the time we end up just guessing what she said or nodding sagely and saying, "Yes." We can tell that she's using actual words rather than jargon, but her pronunciation is so vague that she has to gesture and act things out to get her point across. Obviously, this hasn't affected her confidence so far, but we worry about how things will go when she starts spending more time in groups with other kids. Will they make fun of her? Should we take her to see a speech therapist before then?

A: Your daughter sounds like quite a conversationalist, in her own way! It appears from your description that she is using language skills quite appropriately for her age in several ways. She uses her speech to engage people in social situations, she narrates her everyday activities, she even talks to things that don't talk back. When all else fails, she uses gestures to supplement her requests. The fact that she can't articulate words clearly so that adults always understand her is also quite common at this age. Given how early she started babbling, though, I would be surprised if her articulation doesn't improve quite soon. In the meantime, when she vocalizes, listen carefully to her speech. Pay less attention to the exact pronunciation of the word than to the variety of sounds she makes, her intonation (Does her voice go up when she asks a question, mimicking adult speech?), and whether she makes eye contact during conversations. Read to her and reward her efforts to refine her speech whenever they naturally occur. If you're confident that she hears well and is able to communicate what she wants well enough, don't worry so much about how precise her language is at the moment. Do track her progress, though, and if you're still concerned, make it a priority for your next pediatric visit to discuss whether further steps need to be taken.

TEA AND SYMPATHY: LEARNING TO CONVERSE

Several months have passed, and baby Jacob is struggling to roll over. His older sister, Dana, loves to watch him work at trying to control his brand-new muscles. As she watches him, Jacob looks up at his sister, and his face brightens into a smile. "Mommy! Look!" Dana cries. "Jacob smiling!"

Sharon joins her daughter and laughs at Jacob, trying so hard to charm his sister into picking him up. *It's certainly easier when you can ask with words,* she thinks. She glances at Dana, who has gone back to playing quietly with her dolls and her miniature tea set. It was amazing, once the uproar of a new baby had faded away, how quickly Dana had begun to spout new words. After the first month or so, her feelings about Jacob had seemed to stimulate her desire to speak rather than stifle it. Her sudden interest in imaginary play also seemed to open a new avenue for speech. (Sharon can hear her talking to her dolls even now.) True, she still doesn't chatter away like some of the two-year-olds she plays with, but she talks much more than she did even six weeks ago. Sharon is glad, though, that she discussed her concerns with Dana's doctor. He was able to put her mind at ease, and that took the pressure off both of them.

Sharon's thoughts are interrupted by Jacob's sharp cry. "Oh, Jake!" Dana says before Sharon can respond. "Don't cry." Dana picks up a toy cup and holds it out to her brother. "Want tea?"

ADVANCES
Verbal Achievements in the Second Year

12 MONTHS	May babble in sentences that sound like your language but aren't
	May say two or more words—usually "label" words ("dog"), greetings ("hi," "bye-bye"), or overgeneralized terms ("wa" for water and juice)
	Responds to your simple commands
15 MONTHS	Knows (but probably doesn't yet say) names of people, pets, body parts, favorite objects
	Points to certain objects when you ask her to
	Comprehends many more words than she says
18 MONTHS	Frequently says, "no"

	Vocabulary starts steadily rising
	May refer to herself by name
	May know the names of two colors
	Loves to repeat a word she is learning
21 MONTHS	Uses two-word sentences
	Says "me" and "mine"
	Can name own body parts
	Continues learning new words every day
24 MONTHS	Uses two-, three- and four-word sentences
	Uses "and"
	Uses "I," "me," and "you"
	Says many more words
	Mimics adult inflections, gestures, etc.

FIRST-PERSON SINGULAR

Don't let this year go by without making audiotapes and, if possible, videotapes of your one-year-old's endearing efforts to speak as you do. Not only will you benefit from watching the many ways she works to get her thoughts across to you, but your child will enjoy listening to or watching herself on tape as well, studying her own inflections, her successes and failures at communicating, and your verbal responses. In contrast to her response a year ago, she'll realize that the girl on the screen is her. Two-year-olds enjoy the sounds of their own voice on audiotape at bedtime. Such a tape might ease the going-to-sleep struggle, but she may stay awake a little longer.

Don't forget to record your child's verbal "firsts" here as well. These are some of the most common milestones parents and children want to look back on later. You will probably also want to compare her rate of verbal acquisition to her other cognitive advances later on. Write them down now, before she comes over and starts a conversation.

READER'S NOTES

CHAPTER 5

Tears and Laughter—My Emotional Growth

His frequent outbursts are a result of his disorientation as he struggles with an environment he is only beginning to understand.

It's a beautiful, brisk autumn morning, and Carla has taken Victor, her one-year-old, to the playground. It's crowded there today. Babies sit wide-eyed on grown-ups' laps, toddlers try to climb up the little kids' slides, and older children run shouting to and fro. Carla parks her stroller near an empty bench, unbuckles Victor and sets him on his feet. "Go play," she says cheerfully, and sits down on the bench to keep an eye on him. Though he has only been walking for about a month, Victor is happy with the "long leash" his mother gives him. He has an adventurous temperament and loves to go exploring on his own.

Tentatively, Victor takes a few steps toward the center of the play area. A large red autumn leaf has fallen onto the pavement. Victor is fascinated by its gradations of color and wants to pick it up. He takes one step and then another, concentrating fiercely despite the noise of children playing nearby. Finally he is only a step or two from the leaf. Its colors are so vivid! It's still wet from last night's rain, and the rainwater makes it glisten in the sun. Victor wants to show it to his mom. He looks back toward the bench. But another woman has moved a baby carriage between Victor and his mother. He can't see her!

In an instant, all Victor's confidence, courage, and curiosity vanish. *Where is Mommy?!* He starts toward the spot where she was, staggers, and falls on his bottom. Strangers rush from all directions, all around him. No one is familiar. He starts to wail.

Just then, the woman with the stroller moves on. There's Carla, sitting on the bench. Still crying, Victor reaches for her. "Sweetheart, what's wrong?" she cries, going over to him. She picks him up and gives him a hug. "See, I'm here," she says. "You're okay."

Victor settles down a bit, comforted by his mother's touch and the sound of her voice. He remains in her arms a moment longer, letting the feelings she gives him of confidence and safety build up inside him. Then, emotionally fortified, he struggles to get free. Now that the bond between his mother and himself has been tested and found still strong, he feels comfortable venturing forth again, ready to explore his world. He sees the leaf and starts toward it—but this time he keeps part of his attention on Mommy's presence.

As your twelve- to twenty-four-month-old learns to maneuver—both literally and figuratively—through the wider world of the toddler, he is bound to experience all the tension, excitement, and discomfort of any "new kid on the block." In an environment that he is only beginning to understand, he will necessarily feel disoriented and out of his depth at times. (His panic may feel much like yours when you lose sight of him momentarily in the supermarket or the playground, though perhaps even more unsettling, since he doesn't have the experience to know that the situation will probably be resolved.) His frequent confusion and constant new discoveries this year will cause him to display an entire range of emotions—delight, sadness, fury, frustration, joy, and more—often heightened and sometimes unpredictable. You won't always know the reasons for his outbursts, since it's difficult to fully assess the emotional state of a child with limited language skills. But whatever the cause, his emotions will probably not be well modulated. When unhappy about something, most eighteen-month-olds cannot yet limit themselves to a frown or a pout. Instead, they'll start to cry or even erupt in a tantrum over what may actually be a minor frustration. This behavior doesn't mean they're "spoiled" or "difficult." Putting the brakes on their emotions is just a new experience for them, and they will need plenty of practice before they improve.

The good news is that, as the year progresses, your child's emotional world will grow more sophisticated and, to some degree, manageable. Dr. Daniel Stern, author of *Diary of a Baby: What Your Child Sees, Feels, and Experiences,* and others have written eloquently about how one-year-olds increasingly respond not just reflexively to direct experience (such as having a toy snatched away) but to their own and others' emotions as well (Mommy's disapproval when they snatch the toy back). By the end of the year, your little one's tears and laughter may even be inspired by his private thoughts, memories, and dreams. As his emotional life begins to deepen and change in this way, you'll witness the emergence of his unique personality. You'll learn that he is a sensitive, thoughtful child, or an adventurous, even reckless one. You'll realize that he is somewhat fearful or remarkably placid. This "blossoming" of his character is the great reward for the emotional challenges and frustrations that your little one— and his entire family—may have to endure this year. In the months to follow, you will have the pleasure of really getting to know your child, and enjoying all the intricate ways in which your personalities interact.

A PARENT'S STORY
Warm and Cuddly

"When Vicki was about fifteen months old, she started having trouble going to sleep all over again, even though she'd been on a pretty good schedule for months before that," her mother, Jeannine, told me. "She kept trying to get me to stay in the room with her while she fell asleep, but I wanted her to learn how to go to sleep on her own. I had avoided trying to get her to use a security blanket or stuffed animal before, because I'd heard so many stories about kids who'd lost their blankets or worn them to shreds and then were inconsolable. Vicki finally ground me down with her constant whining at bedtime. I reached under her changing table and got out one of the cloth diapers I used to use as a spit-up cloth. I gave that to her to cuddle up with while she listened to a tape of children's songs, and it actually worked pretty well. She got really attached to that diaper over the next few weeks. I didn't care, because I had plenty more to replace it when it got dirty. It helped her settle back down to her routine, and when she started having the occasional tantrum later, her 'blankie' helped calm her and worked great for me, too. I just wish I'd thought about using something replaceable like that long ago."

A LOVE OF SAFETY:
EMOTIONAL PATTERNS IN THE
FIRST YEAR

Since the day he was born, and even before, much of what your child has learned about emotions he learned directly from you. Over and over during the first eventful months of your child's life, you demonstrated that you were there for him by responding promptly to his cry, feeding him when he was hungry, smiling back and talking to him when he smiled at you, and so on. Each successful encounter between the two of you deepened the attachment, bolstering his confidence that you would support him when he needed you and that even if he turned his back on you for a bit, you would be there waiting when he returned. You no doubt watched him experiment with this concept as he began to crawl. He probably enjoyed creeping out of your sight, then crawling back and "finding" you. He enjoyed checking your expression to see if his absence had worried or frightened you. Above all, though, then as now, he wanted to be in control of the leaving; he didn't like *your* disappearing on him at all! Through these games, the two opposing desires of your baby's emotional life—the urge to explore versus the need for a sense of safety—were first examined.

Sometime between seven and nine months of age, your baby became aware of the presence of strangers—that is, the fact that some people were "his" people, to be trusted, while others definitely were not. This realization signaled a major shift in his concept of his world, threatening his newfound sense of safety and reawakening anxieties about whether *you* were in this sea of unfamiliar people and whether you would come when he needed you. Often during this period, he would carefully gauge your reactions to brief separations (such as when you left him with a caregiver) and other potentially emotional situations. If you appeared anxious, he would most likely become anxious, too. If you seemed calm, he might feel somewhat reassured that even if you left, he would be okay. However, he would probably cry for a little while as you left in any case, simply because he was watching his "secure base" walk out of the room. This crying behavior might have been disappointing on some levels, because he was no longer the "cute bundle" who could be passed from person to person, but it has deep roots as a survival tactic.

As your child approached his first birthday, his experiments in leaving you and finding you, his frequent observations of your own emotional responses, and his experiences weathering your own disappearances and returns instilled in him the belief that though you cannot be at his side every second, you will probably be there when he needs you. His level of confidence in this arena determines to a great degree how free he will feel to venture forth and explore his world in his second year. Ideally, he will be able to deal with a bit more distance from you as he progresses through the months to come. As in all dimensions of development, young children vary tremendously in their abilities to tolerate separation, to self-comfort, and to settle down after feeling upset. One handy idea is to leave behind a "token" of your presence (your purse, for example, or some other object that reminds him of cozy times he's spent with you), to help him move toward greater self-reliance.

This gradual shift from dependence toward independence is not just a physical process. As Dr. Judy Dunn has pointed out in her book *The Beginnings of Social Understanding,* your baby is exploring his own emotions as he explores his physical world. At seven to nine months, he studied your face to gauge your emotional response, then responded in a similar way himself. At twelve months, he may begin experimenting with his own feelings about people and events. He responds differently to people and situations depending on whether or not they are familiar. He demonstrates attachments to others as well as to you—a great advantage as he approaches the superenergetic toddler phase. He also starts to show that he feels differently from you about some things, and as his tastes become clearer, both of you get to know him even better.

Throughout this second year, your baby will continue to move back and forth between his attachment to you and other significant caregivers and his desire for independence. While the two urges coexist within him, one emotion often activates the other. When your baby feels confident and secure, for example, he sets out exploring. But when he goes too far and loses sight of you, his attachment mechanism is activated, and he must make contact again. Once he has "found you," he settles himself until his confidence returns, and he sets out exploring again. As the months pass, the reassurance he needs shifts from physical touch to eye contact and a smile to a casual acknowledgment as he shows you a toy from across the room. But the road to independence is fraught with pitfalls. There are bound to be times when your little one panics because he feels too far away from you (physically or emotionally), and times when he rebels because he feels you are holding him too close.

Though it is hard sometimes to be aware of where on the spectrum your child happens to be emotionally at the moment—and to make allowances for it amid the clamor of daily life—the more understanding and supportive you can be throughout this challenging period, the better for your child in the long run. His ability to rely on you to be there has been shown again and again in scientific studies to have a real long-term impact on his sense of well-being. One such study with which I was associated, called the Minnesota Parent-Child Project, followed 180 children from birth through age twenty. With comprehensive information on each child's social, cognitive, and emotional development, including his or her temperament, IQ level, and other distinct traits, the researchers found that no matter what their individual differences, the kinds of attachments the children formed with their primary caregivers *at one year of age* predicted: (1) their teacher ratings, behavior problems, and quality of relationships with peers in preschool (2) their social competency as ten- and eleven-year-olds in summer camp, (3) their ability to empathize with others as they grew older, (4) their resilience in the face of personal difficulties, and (5) their school achievement level as teenagers.

A BABY'S-EYE VIEW
A Friend Indeed

Strangers, twelve-month-old Tony thinks as the people enter his house. The smells, sounds, and shapes of these newcomers alert him that they do not belong here. Mommy looks happy as she ushers them inside. *Why is she looking at them and not at me?* Tony holds his arms up for his mom. "Uh!" he grunts. He knows the word "up," but at times when he feels uneasy it doesn't always come out right. He wants Mommy to pick him up and cuddle him. "Uh!"

Finally Mommy notices Tony. She smiles and picks him up. "There you are, big boy," she says. Tony feels better. But then she turns her face away again! "Look how big he's gotten," she says proudly to the strange ones. Tony looks warily at their big, unfamiliar faces all leaning forward, staring at him. *Go away!* he thinks. He starts to cry.

"May I hold him?" one of the strangers says. She reaches out for Tony. At the touch of her hands, he starts to scream. *Mommy!* he wants to say, *Make her stop!*

Now Mommy is frowning. "I don't know what's wrong with him. He's usually friendlier." She hands him to the stranger.

Help! Tony feels as though his ties to Mommy have just been snapped. He struggles in the stranger's arms. The unfamiliar texture of her clothes rubs irritatingly against him. *Must have Mommy!* He feels himself losing control. His fear washes over him, and he starts to scream and kick.

"Okay, Tony, here I am." Mommy's arms are suddenly around him. He feels safe again. He snuggles against her and relishes the sense of warmth and security. A moment later, as Mommy carries him into the living room, he peeks over her shoulder. *Who are these new people anyway? They're all smiling and laughing. Oh. One is carrying a stuffed bear. Hmm. Nice bear,* he thinks as his eyes follow it across the room.

THE AGE OF DISCOVERY:
EMOTIONAL GROWTH IN THE
SECOND YEAR

Your one-year-old's first steps out into the world are a poignant reminder that sometime around the beginning of his second year, he has begun to realize that the two of you are not one indivisible unit. Increasingly, as he begins walking on his own two feet and thinking about the world around him in terms of words and ideas (rather than just responding instinctively to each sensation), he plays with the notion that his own mood, emotions, and thoughts can be separate, and even different, from yours. An interesting experiment by Dr. Joseph Campos and his colleagues demonstrated this change in perspective for the developing child. Babies of different ages were encouraged to crawl across a flat Plexiglas surface (called a "visual cliff") with what looked like a sharp, steplike drop underneath. As far as the babies could tell, they would tumble over the edge of the step if they continued crawling forward. When the babies were around nine months old, they would crawl toward the apparent drop-off, see the "step," and start to turn around to descend the step backward—but if they saw their mothers smiling encouragingly at them, they would change their minds and crawl blithely ahead, over the drop, instead. (If their mothers instead looked suddenly anxious or frightened, the babies would stop in their tracks.) After twelve months, on the other hand, some babies would note their mothers' reactions, hesitate while they weighed their mothers' assessments of the danger against their own, and then, even if their mothers were smiling, would turn around to descend the step backward. In other words, though the older babies still looked to their mothers to gauge their emotional responses, they no longer automatically shared them.

In the 1980s, Dr. Megan Gunnar of the University of Minnesota devised an experiment in which twelve- to thirteen-month-olds were shown three toys, one frightening, one pleasant, and one "ambiguous"—that is, it could be frightening or pleasant, depending on one's attitude. Gunnar found that the one-year-olds checked their mothers' responses to the toys before playing with them. If their mothers smiled encouragingly, the babies would play with the ambiguous toys, but they would not play with the frightening toys even if their mothers looked unafraid and encouraging. Again, these children were interested in their mothers' emotional responses but did not always mimic them.

When he is between twelve and fifteen months of age, your own child's emotional state will revolve around this amazing, dawning realization—that he has his thoughts and you have your thoughts, and they might not always be the same. The idea of emotional separateness is truly mind-boggling for a child who until recently assumed that you and he were in some sense a single whole. During this time, you will see him start to test your emotional responses to his own and others' actions, not only to determine how he himself should feel but to see whether you feel the same way he does.

Still, during this period, when motor development is so dramatic, there is not as much energy available for examining feelings as there will be later in the year. Your child is beginning to very roughly "feel out the emotional territory" in his newly discovered separate self—but only when he isn't distracted by his efforts to get the bleach bottle off the shelf in the laundry room or to stagger at top speed down the sidewalk just out of your reach. Until about eighteen months, much of his emotional life still centers on his own physical activity. He sees something (a bird or a cat) and is filled with a determination to catch it. He laughs with pleasure when he falls down on purpose, rocks on a rocking horse, pounds on things, or throws toys around.

Between eighteen and twenty-one months, however, as his focus on motor activity begins to relax, he starts to notice more what your own responses are to his activity. It may dawn on him at this point that though he finds it quite amusing to drop the entire contents of your jewelry box into the dog's water bowl, you don't seem to think it's so funny. Over the next few months, he becomes increasingly fascinated by this disparity between your responses and his own. He begins to get a keener sense of what's expected and unexpected. Over time, he figures out that if he changes his behavior, your (and others') responses will change. This is a wonderful discovery for toddlers, who so desperately yearn to control their limited environment. You may chuckle as you watch him reach his hand toward the hot-water faucet in the bathtub, then pull away, then reach for it, then pull away—while staring fascinated (as in the crawling-off-the-step experiment) at your mouth turning down and up, down and up. But you are experiencing a wonderful early opportunity to show your toddler how to behave. Make it clear to him now, in gentle, informative, consistent, nonpunitive ways, what you expect from him in specific situ-

Emotional outbursts can be avoided by letting your toddler experiment, under close supervision.

ations (such as brushing his teeth twice a day, putting on his pajamas at night, going to sleep once the lights are out, and holding your hand when he crosses the street), and you may avoid a lot of conflict later on.

During this period, your toddler's cognitive (thinking) and affective (feeling) skills are deeply intertwined. The more he is aware of his separateness from others, the more sensitive he can become to the feelings of others. Gradually, his understanding will grow sufficiently to target and predict others' feelings with some accuracy. This is why, after snatching a toy from another child's hand, your eighteen-month-old will stare in fascination at the crying child without looking particularly sorry or even sympathetic, while at twenty-four months he may try to remedy the situation or even burst into tears himself. Within that six-month span he has begun to empathize—that is, to understand, not just recognize, others' emotions. His empathy may also prompt him to hug you when you're feeling blue or even tell you fondly that he "wuvs" you when you sing a happy song or do something funny to amuse him. This development comes as quite a relief to those parents (and there are many) who've had to fend off fears that they were raising a rather chilly person during those earlier months, but evolution from emotional experimenter to empathizer is quite natural.

As your child approaches his second birthday, you will see him interact emotionally with others on an increasingly sophisticated level. His social and emotional development has now reached a more complex stage. "I can't believe the difference," one mother told me. "A year ago, he pretty much depended on *us* to control his emotions. If he was frightened, *we* needed to fix it. Now he's so much better at calming himself down when he's upset or even soothing his baby brother." It's true—your two-year-old has assumed his place as a unique member of your family. He may pretend to take a bite out of the table to amuse you, offer to share a toy with his brother, and laugh with delight at the cartoon characters playing happily on TV. He has entered a generally sunny time for children altogether, in fact—a rewarding plateau after the steady climb from an undifferentiated "oneness" toward proud individuality.

THE TOY BOX
If I Had a Hammer . . .

At eighteen months, Max can go over to his toy box and pull out his favorite toy all by himself, thank you. He rummages around until he finds the plastic animal noisemaker. Confidently, he punches one of the big plastic buttons, and the toy barks like a dog. He punches another. The toy moos. This is old stuff for Max now.

Dad walks into the room in his bathrobe, settling down on the couch to read the paper. Max waits for him to play, but Dad hasn't had his first cup of coffee yet. Max thinks for a moment. Then he pounds his plastic toy on the floor, making a big, satisfying bang. The newspaper slams down, and there's Daddy, looking at him!

"Max!" says Daddy loudly. Max laughs impishly. He slams the toy on the floor again. Daddy frowns even more. "I said stop that, Max!"

This is fascinating. Every time Max pounds the toy on the

floor, Daddy looks at him and says something. He sounds angry! As soon as Daddy has started reading the paper again, Max crosses the room toward him. He stops a couple of feet away, hesitates, then pounds the plastic toy—just a little less hard—on the coffee table.

The newspaper slams down again! Max watches in wide-eyed anticipation. Daddy starts to yell, then manages to restrain himself. "Don't hit the table," he says instead, still annoyed. "You'll hurt the table and break your toy. If you want to pound something, I'll get your hammer and pegs. Come on." Seeing that his son looks apprehensive, he gently removes the toy from his hand and adds, as he sets up the new game, "Tell you what. After I've had my coffee, we can go work on that bench I'm building for the backyard. You can help Daddy, okay?"

Max takes the toy hammer from his father. He didn't understand everything Daddy said, but he liked his tone better. He glances toward the coffee table. It would be fun to hit it, but he knows Daddy would really get mad if he did. *Daddy said "yard,"* he thinks. Max heads for the back door, toy hammer in hand—not willing to wait for coffee.

"IS THIS CHILD *MINE*?": YOUR CHILD'S TEMPERAMENT

"I don't know what to do about him," I overheard a mother confess to a friend in the children's play area of a pediatrician's waiting room recently. She had her two-year-old son in an iron grip as he was struggling to get free. A few feet away, the mother of a younger child was trying to comfort her while inspecting the bite the boy had just given her. To her credit, the boy's mother looked just as distressed as everyone else who had witnessed the incident. "He's always been this way," she said to her friend. "I don't know why he always acts so angry. It's not like we ever spank him. We hardly ever even raise our voices at home!"

Often parents express bewilderment over how their children "got that way"—both in a negative sense and in other ways, as with a child who is sociable and friendly though his parents are painfully shy. Developmental psychologists, including Dr. Jerome Kagan of Harvard University, point out that this basic emotional makeup—called *temperament*—is essentially part of a child's genetic inheritance and is separate from his life experience. Precisely because it is out of their control, temperament is a source of some of parents' greatest fears and greatest pleasures—in a sense, it really is the great parental lottery. Your child's natural rhythms, his level of activity, his sociability or lack thereof, his general optimism or pessimism are all largely determined (and even, in some cases, expressed) before he is born. Equally important, however, is how well his temperament fits with yours, how well you are "attuned" to his general emotional state, and how successfully you are managing to work with his basic temperament in ways that are good for him. In other words, nature is a vital key in determining what sort of personality your child has, but "nurture" plays at least as great (if not greater) a role in your child's behavior.

Certainly every parent-child combination is unique. Some mothers are fortunate enough to have given birth to a child they understand perfectly and who "understands" them. Parent and child are able to communicate and get along together without really having to think about it. Other mother-child couples seem somehow out of sync. You may not feel quite comfortable and secure with your child, or he may not feel that way with you. As did the mother in the waiting room, you may even feel embarrassed or shocked by your child's apparent temperament and expressed behavior, finding that you don't even like him at times. This is a sad situation and a difficult one. But it is not your child's fault, nor your own. If you find yourself in this position, it's important to assess the situation as objectively as possible, examine the ways you can change your child's environment to gradually shape the ways in which his temperament is expressed, and try as much as possible to make clear that it's his behavior (and not him) that you dislike.

If your eighteen-month-old has started biting children on the playground, it doesn't mean he's bad or that you are a bad parent. Difficult as it is to keep in mind when other parents are throwing disapproving looks your way, the fact is that the second year is a time when children naturally experiment with all kinds of behavior just to find out what kinds of responses they will create. In fact, no matter how much you "like" your child or how good the relationship is, this is an age that tends to be difficult for everyone. Your child is active enough to create all kinds of emotional drama, yet he has not yet reached that empathic stage when he completely understands how his actions make others feel. So when your one-year-old behaves badly, don't be too quick to decide that that's "just the way he is." Your child is still in an extreme state of flux. Many of his apparent personality traits, such as stubbornness, selfishness, and negativity, may really be just phases that every child goes through and that will fade away if you don't pay too much attention to them. Even the more permanent aspects of his character are open to parental guidance and "retuning." So don't judge his character or assign him particular characteristics too early (as in, "Reed's such a *loud* boy").

It also makes sense to keep in mind that just because this child is very different from his brother, his sister, or the child next door, that doesn't mean he's better than or inferior to the other child. Each child is different, with a fascinating mix of good and bad traits that are continuously reshaped by his life experience (much like us adults). In addition, many children create a first impression that is very different from how they really are. Your child may put people off at first with his apparent hyperactivity, but those who know him better understand that he is just a very exuberant, happy child.

Whatever your child's temperament—whether he talks a mile a minute, spends much of his time contentedly puttering about on his own, gets unnervingly "physical" with kids he's just met, or leaves the room the instant a new person enters—try to drop your own assumptions for a moment and see the world from his point of view. He may not be the typical kind of person you'd pick to be your friend (he may chatter all day when you'd rather read a book), but he is a one-of-a-kind individual with his own strengths and his own worth. Sharing his childhood with him means you'll get to know a person "like him"—a type of person you'd ordinarily never mix with—in a very intimate way. Giving him a chance to express himself in your presence allows you to show your appreciation and respect for him and will give you ideas for ways to channel his negative energy into more positive outlets. As he grows, he will deeply appreciate this effort at attunement and will repay you a thousandfold with his own respect and desire to do well. If he is truly a challenging child by nature, he will need your understanding and patience more than ever. Look at it as your best shot at unconditional love.

Try as they might, it has been difficult for developmental psychologists to tease out precisely where inherited temperament ends in an infant and where environmentally influenced traits begin. Certainly, as any mother of twins or more than one child can tell you, there are obvious behavioral differences among babies even in utero. From the moment of birth, some cry a lot, some are quiet, some sleep regularly, others wake at all hours. Though it is also possible to "create" irritable or active babies by interacting with them in particular ways, babies are undeniably biased toward certain moods and emotions. However, the fact is that practically from the first encounter, parents react to what they perceive as the infant's temperament and change their own behavior accordingly. If a baby smiles and makes plenty of eye contact with his parents, they tend to smile and make eye contact back. If he sleeps most of the time or looks away frequently, the parents may not interact with him as much. This shaping mechanism continues as the child grows older. A study designed by pioneering researchers Drs. Alexander Thomas and Stella Chess demonstrated that mothers of twelve-month-olds responded similarly to their babies whether they were categorized as "difficult" or "easy" but exerted far less effort in trying to control the difficult children as little as six months later. It pays to be aware of this tendency to adjust to a baby's apparent character and change your responses when they aren't productive.

One way to work at managing the "mutual shaping" process so that it works in your and your child's best interests is to be aware of behaviors that are typical of a particular age and are therefore probably not specifically due to your child's basic temperament. If you can avoid reacting too much to these temporary behavior patterns, they will eventually settle down. In the second year, your child's most challenging time is likely to fall somewhere between age fifteen and twenty-one months. During this period, he is old enough to formulate very strong desires but isn't always able to satisfy them. This clearly creates frustration and leads to all kinds of difficult behavior, including shouts of "No!," refusals to cooperate with your wishes, and outright tantrums. Frankly, much of this behavior is part of the territory for this phase of his life. Your best response is to do what you can to gently curb his excesses (by refusing to give in to overly rude demands, by modeling and discussing appropriate ways to express his anger, and especially by avoiding frustrating scenarios whenever possible) and to remind yourself that this behavior isn't going to last forever. Remember that a child needs to try out *all* his new feelings, negative as well as positive. In fact, he will probably save his most intense feelings (good and bad) for you. This is why, even after a placid day with his caregiver, he will completely disintegrate when you arrive, behaving as though he's not happy to see you. Depressing as that can feel when it's happening, keep in mind that he's actually demonstrating the strength of his love for you, using his sense of safety with you to have the meltdown he was holding back all day. "My mother used to give me such a look when I picked Carl up from her house after work, when he was around one and a half," one mother told me. "A lot of the time he'd see me and just start screaming. My mom would say something like 'We did nothing but laugh and play all day.' After I realized that he was just letting go of all his pent-up feelings at once, I felt a lot better about it, and he stopped doing it soon enough."

IF YOU'RE CONCERNED
Your "Challenging" Child

The second year is a particularly difficult time to tell if your child is just "going through a phase" or if he is dealing with a more lasting emotional (or behavioral) challenge. If you have been worrying that he seems overly aggressive, angry, frustrated, listless, or reclusive, even for his age, confront your feelings now and begin researching their validity. One way to do this would be to ask others who know your child for an honest reading. Do they believe that he has a problem or that he's just acting like a typical toddler? Next, monitor your own responses to his questionable behavior. Do you aggravate the situation—making too big a deal out of his refusal to cooperate, for example—and thus reinforce his actions through your increased attention? In many cases, his behavior may simply be a case of being exposed too often to the triggers that happen to set him off. Pay attention to what time of day he usually falls into the behavior pattern that worries you. Does he begin "acting that way" when he hasn't eaten for several hours, when he's missed his nap, when he's in a room with a lot of other children? Correcting his behavior may be just a matter of avoiding those "trigger" situations whenever possible.

In the meantime, keep in mind that a "challenging" child, as Dr. Stanley Greenspan, co-author of *The Challenging Child: Understanding, Raising, and Enjoying the Five "Difficult" Types of Children,* terms such children, is not directing his behavior at you but is responding to stress at some level within himself. Sensitive or very active children can have particular trouble during this year, when they must deal with so much internal change. Failed interaction with others his age will only lead to more frustration in the future, so it's best to try to deal with the causes of his misbehavior now, before his world widens even more.

"NO!":
DEALING WITH TANTRUMS

Alisha had been taking her daughter, Maia, to a child-care center near her workplace since Maia was six months old. From the beginning, Maia seemed to enjoy the center, and Alisha was confident in the quality of care that her daughter received there. Whenever Alisha dropped in for a visit at lunchtime or came to pick Maia up, Maia was busily engaged in an activity by herself, with other children, or with one of the caregivers. Alisha especially enjoyed reading the daily summary of Maia's activities and accomplishments. One day, though, when Maia was about twenty months old, something went wrong. Alisha took her to the child-care center in her stroller, as usual, but when they reached the front door, Maia refused to get out of the stroller and go inside. "No!" she wailed as Alisha tried to pull her out of her seat. Her cries were so loud they made Alisha's ears ring, and the other parents stared as they passed by with their own (well-behaved) children. Mortified, Alisha asked Maia to lower her voice. But Maia was oblivious to the effect she was having on everyone else; she was completely caught up in the feeling of panic she was experiencing. Alisha tried asking Maia what was wrong, to no avail. She mentally reviewed the summary of Maia's activities from yesterday, but nothing seemed out of the ordinary. In the end, Alisha had no choice but to pick Maia up and carry her into the child-care center. After checking in with the teacher, she left Maia with a promise to call later. "I feel like the worst parent on the planet," she told me over the phone from work. "I feel like I'll never be able to set foot in that center again."

Of course, as Alisha learned when she returned to pick Maia up that day, the child-care workers had seen far worse tantrums than that one in their careers. Maia was her old cheerful self by then, throwing herself affectionately on her mother as soon as she saw her. Alisha was relieved as she hugged her little girl to know that she had kept her own temper in check sufficiently during the tantrum not to have said anything damaging that she would now regret. Reviewing the situation on the ride home, Alisha decided that the tantrum must have resulted from the rush they had been in that morning. Everyone had overslept, and Maia had been snatched out of bed and jammed into her clothes without her usual wake-up routine. Then they realized that they were out of the raisin bread that Maia liked for breakfast. Finally, it was raining, and Maia had had to sit inside the plastic stroller cover, which she hated. As a result, she'd passed her frustration threshold and just disintegrated.

Alisha knew she could expect rough drop-offs and pickups from the child-care center occasionally, but she never wanted to go through another tantrum like that one first thing in the morning. She made plans to avoid future tantrums before they happened. "I tried waking Maia a little earlier for the rest of the week, to give her time to awaken gradually," she told me. "It's amazing what a difference that little change made. She's never had another tantrum like that one. I just didn't realize how out-of-control any little change in her routine made her feel at that age. Now I make sure we have extra raisin bread, just in case!"

Experts generally agree that a tantrum is your child's way of telling you when he's reached his limit of frustration and needs you to help him make things right. Usually resulting from the gap between his desire to do something (grab a handful of candy at the grocery-store checkout, for example) and his ability to do it, this frustration builds until he is unable to express it in any other way. Tantrums at this age are in no way signs that your child is "spoiled" or that you are a bad parent. They are simply symptoms of your child's development as he learns to cope with a complex new set of feelings.

One of the worst aspects of a tantrum is its potential to embarrass the parent, but there's no need to suffer unduly if and when your child has a tantrum in a public place. You can be sure that the large majority of people passing by (or even glaring disapprovingly at you) have been or will be in exactly the same situation one of these days. Hard as it is, one of your primary challenges is not to let your embarrassment lead you to "punish" your child. Spanking him, telling him he's acting like a baby, yelling, or otherwise getting highly emotional yourself will only make matters worse. Right now, he needs to know you're the "rock" he can cling to as he tries to find his bearings. He can only climb out of his chaotic state if you remind him (through your own behavior) what it feels like to be calm.

Children respond differently to various comfort techniques, so you may have to try several before you figure out how you can best calm your out-of-control child. If you're at home, you have the option of letting him work out his emotions himself. Either pick him up and hold him quietly or gather him up and carry him to a safe spot where he can cry and kick to his heart's content. Then go about your business while checking in verbally once in a while ("Are you feeling better, Patrick? Would you like me to read you a story?"). Basically, he needs to figure out how to get control of himself again, and there's not much more you can do to help him. Moving away from him may also help you resist the very real temptation to go over the edge yourself. You are in more danger of behaving in ways you'll later regret at home where no one is watching. If necessary, leave him for a few moments until you're sure you've regained control.

In public places, it's important to stop the noise as soon as possible. Of course, the best solution to these tantrums is to try to avoid them in the first place. But if your child loses it, perhaps it's best just to concentrate on getting him out of there as quickly as possible. (Try to avoid well-meaning strangers who try to help and may foil your escape.) As you hustle your child out of there, remind yourself that this, too, shall pass. Later, when everyone's calmed down, try to figure out what might have caused the tantrum. Often it's a minor occurrence that you never would have suspected meant so much to your child. One father who loved to take his one-year-old grocery-shopping after work had a wonderful time picking out vegetables and treats with her, but each time they reached the checkout area, she fell into a tantrum for no reason he could understand. Finally he realized that the moment when he was unloading the grocery cart onto the conveyer belt was the only time he turned his back on her. Apparently this made his daughter feel suddenly alone and lost. As soon as her father learned to face her as he unloaded groceries, her behavior cleared up. When such behavior inevitably happens, ask yourself what's different in the way you or your child approached the situation. You might come up with a clue that could prevent future episodes.

EASING THE WAY

Avoiding Tantrums

Tantrums are extremely unpleasant for parent, child, and anyone else within earshot. The best way to avoid them is, as always, to think ahead a little. The first rule in preventing an uncontrollable level of frustration from building up in your child is to stick to his daily routine as much as possible. If he is used to having lunch at noon and then taking a short nap, delaying lunch or the nap will raise his stress level. When you do need to change the order or occurrence of his usual activities, inform him ahead of time and be ready to fall back to a simpler schedule (such as skipping the trip to the library or having a quieter than usual afternoon). Transitions are another common situation that is hard on toddlers. Try to move from one activity to another gradually, rather than just placing your child abruptly in another environment, among a new group of people, or even in a new outfit without warning. Sometimes toddlers lose control because they feel they are over-restricted. (That's why strollers, grocery carts, and car seats are often the places where things erupt.) Try giving your little one as much freedom as possible to explore his world without placing him in physical danger. Finally, when he absolutely refuses to go along with your wishes, ask yourself what the long-term goal is and aim for that. For instance, if you want to give him a bath but he refuses to take off his underwear, ask yourself what's more important—taking off his underwear or the bath? There's nothing fundamentally wrong with letting him wear his underwear in the bath once or twice so he can find out what it's like. That way he will have figured out that it's not really much fun, and you won't have had to fight about it.

Many tantrums can be avoided or alleviated just by maintaining awareness of your child's level of maturity and specific skills—in other words, how much change, challenge, and "strangeness" he can take. If you learn to recognize the signs that he is about to lose control, you may be able to distract or comfort him before the yelling starts. Positive reinforcement during the good times works very well, too. When he's been particularly well behaved say, "I'm proud you're being so patient waiting your turn." (Not, "You're a good boy for being so patient.") He may remember your praise and strive to hear it again on a more challenging day.

A WIN-WIN SITUATION: LETTING THE OTHER PARENT PARENT, TOO

Mothers are of vital importance in one-year-olds' busy lives, but don't forget that fathers and other male caregivers can also contribute a great deal. Landmark research by Dr. Ross Parke of the University of California at Riverside and Dr. Michael Lamb, author of *The Father's Role: Cross-Cultural Perspectives,* has focused particularly on what fathers bring to families. The results indicate that fathers' involvement in their babies' caretaking leads to gains in the babies' cognitive and emotional development. School-age children whose fathers spent a higher than average amount of time with them as infants have been shown to have significantly higher IQ scores, longer attention spans, more eagerness for learning, and even more of a sense of humor than those whose fathers did not participate. In his recent book, *Fatherneed: Why Father Care Is as Essential as Mother Care for Your Child,* Dr. Kyle Pruett of Yale University points out that fathers help enrich their children's self-image and contribute to a more stable family-support structure for the child. Looking ahead, father in-

Nothing can ease your toddler's anxiety like the security provided by loving, involved parents.

volvement in the teenage years gives the adolescent a stronger sense of his inner "locus of control"—the ability to resist peer pressure because he is sure of his own values.

Certainly, having a helpful partner around can greatly lower the stress level in your household. Involved partners can also temper the intensity of the mother-infant relationship once your child is ready to become a little more independent. Finally, any two caregivers are bound to have different approaches to raising a baby. It helps a developing child to witness a variety of behavior patterns and interact with adults in different ways—as long as the adults don't argue incessantly about whose approach is better.

Some dads are completely natural, involved caregivers, but especially with a first child, dads are subject to the same insecurities and misconceptions as moms are. As you watch him toss your baby up in the air (practically giving you a heart attack as the child's head almost touches the ceiling) and order him to clean up his toy closet (when he's obviously much too young), keep in mind that your partner may not have had all those years of baby-sitting experiences, conversations with his mother about child care, talks with pediatricians, and other experiences that have traditionally prepared many women for parenthood. He may well feel self-conscious as he tries to establish his separate relationship with his child—especially if you're watching him every second. Surely you can empathize with his feelings when your child screams for you and (at least for the moment) rejects him. Support him in his continued efforts, resisting the temptation to criticize but making yourself available for advice if he asks for it. The rewards—a more cohesive family, a more secure child, and someone to talk to about that fascinating child—are worth the effort.

Q & A
She Doesn't Want Me . . .

Q: When my wife became pregnant, we agreed that I would take on half of the parenting duties whenever possible. I have tried to do that, but from the beginning, my one-year-old daughter has preferred her mom to me. When I try to take her for the afternoon, she whines that she wants to be with Mommy. When I go in to tell her bedtime stories, she refuses to let me. What am I doing wrong?

A: Regardless of dads' good intentions, infants' attachment to their primary caregivers, who in this society tend to be the mothers, is so strong that sharing the child-care duties can sometimes be difficult. Some babies and toddlers resist being "passed off" to Daddy at first, and they aren't usually very tactful about expressing their preferences. Too often this resistance causes dads to throw up their hands and retreat in frustration to the office or the TV set. This is a real shame, because a relationship with your child is vitally important for you, for her, and for the family's health. If you can, try to overlook your little one's stubborn resistance to changing hands. Make a point of doing some of your child's favorite activities together (not just the chores), so that she will learn that time with Dad is often fun time. Taking on some of the more serious responsibilities of parenting, such as bringing your child to the pediatrician for her checkups, may also add more dimension to your relationship with your child. If you are unsure about some aspect of parenting, you can talk with the doctor or with other actively involved parents, as well as your wife, about effective methods that have worked for them.

It might help to know that as they grow, young children throw their allegiance back and forth from one parent to another, each time with great passion and loyalty. Your little one may be Mommy's baby now, but—as I overheard one father of a four-year-old assuring a toddler girl's dad at a child's birthday party the other day—"Don't worry, pal, your time will come."

AND THE CAREGIVER MAKES FOUR: EXPANDING YOUR CHILD'S FAMILY

As the months pass, your child's world will continue to widen to include more caregivers, friends, and other family members. It is good to know that no matter how many people he learns to love, there's always enough love to go around. A great deal of recent research, including a seminal long-term study published in 1997 by the National Institute for Child Health and Development, has shown that quality child care does not affect the security of a baby's attachment to his parents. In other words, babies don't confuse the caregivers in their lives or choose only one person to whom to attach themselves. Your child will always know and appreciate the fact that you are his mom or dad. Of course, it is sometimes easier to *tell* yourself that your baby will always love you most than it is to believe it when he starts screaming the moment you challenge his desire to stay and play with his caregiver. Remember that, as any parent can tell you, children this age routinely save up their emotional demonstrations until the moment they can unload them on their parents—and that his "show" is one way of telling you how much you mean to him. Count yourself lucky that your child *is* so attached to his caregiver. Think about how sad his life would be if he were not! For your own mental health and your child's sake, try not to compete with your caregiver—or allow her to compete with you—over who is the best "parent" to your little one. Focus instead on your shared love for him and on what you can learn from each other about how to deal with the behavioral challenges that arise.

Oddly, parents sometimes forget how important a particular caregiver can become to a one-year-old, no matter how temporary they assumed that caregiver to be. Transitions from one caregiving situation to another can be very upsetting to your child, as difficult for him as you might find moving to a new house in your own life. When possible, it's best to phase out one caregiver gradually and phase in the next, so that there's a time when your child spends time with each of the participants and doesn't experience an abrupt transition. Be sure to talk about the change with him ahead of time, while it's happening, and afterward—keeping in mind the fact that he can understand many more words than he can say. Even the transition from the babies' room to the completely different and initially strange toddlers' room at the child-care center can throw him out of balance. As his second year progresses, make sure that any such transitions are handled with tact and an awareness of your child's very real emotional attachments.

Where Did She Go?

Q: My twenty-month-old son, Luke, was very close to his full-time sitter, Andrea, who began taking care of him when he was four months old. He cried when she left at the end of each day, so much that I had to work hard to keep from feeling jealous. Two months ago, Andrea's family suddenly had to move back to their native country. We told Luke she was leaving, of course, but I'm not sure he really understood. Now that she's gone, he keeps asking where she is, and I don't know what to tell him. How can I help him deal with Andrea's not being in his life anymore?

A: Changes in relationships are hard for everyone, but this is especially true for toddlers. Your son's asking for his caregiver is only natural, given the strong relationship they shared for most of his life to date. Frankly, at this age, preparing him for her sudden departure was probably all you could do at the time. Now, though, there are several ways to help make this physical loss of a special person a bit easier for him (and you!). Continue to talk about Andrea routinely or when your son asks for her, keep photos of her nearby and refer to them visually, even after you have a new caregiver in place. When he colors a picture, tell him you're going to send it to her, and let him help you mail it. He won't understand the logistics of distance or how long it will be before he sees her again, but he will make the connection between talking about her, seeing her face, and his happy associations with her. If at all possible, an occasional phone call would be a wonderful opportunity to hear her voice again and strengthen that connection. As hard as it is, think of this separation as an important lesson in life—that special people come and go in ways we cannot control but physical distance does not mean that important relationships have to end.

"SEE YOU LATER!":
EXPANDING THE EMOTIONAL
BOUNDARIES

Frank, the little boy down the street, is just two weeks younger than Victor, and today is his second birthday party. Carla and Victor have been invited, and they are pleased to visit Frank's house for the first time. When they arrive, Carla ushers Victor into the playroom with the other children. She sees that several parents she knows have already taken charge of monitoring the room, so after lingering for a while until she sees that Victor is comfortable, she gives him a quick, reassuring wave and she slips out of the room to grab a soda.

A brief time later, Carla peeks back into the playroom. She finds the kids all gathered around Frank's dad, who is blowing up balloons. Carla watches Victor stand with the other children, entranced by the sight of so many balloons. A balloon pops. Victor looks startled, and a child next to him starts to cry. Carla watches Victor give the crying child a concerned look. Then he sticks his thumb in his mouth, soothing himself as Frank's dad comforts the crying child and starts blowing up another balloon.

What a difference, Carla thinks. A year ago Victor could hardly let her out of his sight. Now he has learned all kinds of ways to manage his emotions. *He's becoming so independent,* Carla thinks as she smiles across the room at an adult acquaintance. Sometimes it's nice for grown-ups to enjoy some independence, too.

ADVANCES
Emotional Achievements in the Second Year

12 MONTHS   Emotional states tend to vary easily

Is easily distracted from source of discomfort

Enjoys looking at himself in the mirror

Begins to understand that his feelings are separate from his parents'

May mirror others' emotions

15 MONTHS

May experiment with sharing, but then want object back

May cry often but is easily comforted by a loved one

May notice when familiar people are missing

Starts to prefer certain clothes and routines

18 MONTHS

Becomes easily frustrated

Finds it difficult to manage his emotions

Acts impulsively

Uses blanket, stuffed animal, or favorite toy to comfort himself

21 MONTHS

Begins to recognize others' emotions

Expresses love for parents through hugging, etc.

Starts to understand concept of "good" and "bad" behavior

Makes some attempts to control crying

24 MONTHS

Is generally less impulsive

Thrives on a reliable routine

Can be bossy at times

Self-confidence has increased

Takes pride in doing things himself

FIRST-PERSON SINGULAR

As you watch your one-year-old grow more independent and learn to recognize and manage his own emotions, take some time to write down your observations here. What was his confidence level on his first play date? His fifth? How did he and you weather that change in caregivers? What is his favorite comfort object? How has he learned to show you he loves you? Who are his favorite people? What activities does he particularly enjoy doing with Dad?

It is fun to look back at these notes later and see which traits turned out to be a part of your child's ongoing personality and which were just a sign of a temporary phase. Though difficult to see at the time, these differences eventually become very clear.

READER'S NOTES

_____

_____

_____

_____

_____

_____

_____

_____

_____

_____

_____

_____

CHAPTER 6

Where I Stand—My Social Development

She's learning to share experiences and compare her reactions with others'.

A new family has moved in next door, and Marian and Bill have invited them over for dinner. Marian is glad they're bringing their two-year-old son, Pete, as well. Her own daughter, Clara, hasn't had much experience with other children, since she's an only child and only twelve months old. Marian looks forward to watching her daughter play with a brand-new friend.

Pete turns out to be a very nice boy, and Marian and Bill like his parents, too. As the adults drink coffee after dinner, Marian turns Clara loose to practice her walking skills in the dining room. Bill has already brought the toy box into the dining room, so Pete will have plenty of things to play with.

Constantly admonished by his parents to "be nice to Clara," and "show Clara the toy," Pete does try to interest the one-year-old in playing with him. But Clara brushes right past him, focused on her movement and determined to walk all the way across the room. Most of the time, the two children don't even seem to notice each other; each is absorbed in his or her own activity. "Mommy, look!" Pete says, going to his mother, holding up one of Clara's toys to show her. "Turtle!"

Distracted from her walking by the sound of Pete's voice, Clara turns to see Pete holding aloft one of her toys. He's heading toward *her* parents (it seems) with *her* toy! Clara lets out a yell of protest. She heads straight for Pete, clearly intending to get back the toy. Sighing, Marian and Bill both get up to deal with her. Obviously, Clara is no good at winning friends and influencing people. *Will she ever learn?* Marian wonders.

The fact is, social skills with peers are not a top-priority aspect of development for this young a child, compared to the obvious need to form attachments to Mom and Dad. Though children in this country seem to develop certain social skills earlier now than in previous generations, your one-year-old is not likely to start appreciating the joys of friendship until the end of her second year or even later. In general, your child will move from a preoccupation with *physical* skills toward *psychological* issues. She needs to proceed in her development from the inside (her own body and feelings) out (her relationships with others). She demonstrates this not only in her behavior but through her body language; most infants' first "bye-bye" wave is directed inward, as though waving to themselves, but over the year they turn their pudgy hands around and start greeting the outside world.

Your child cannot progress far in her social skills until she begins to come to grips with the distinction between herself and others. This important step generally occurs in the first half of the second year. As she gradually comes to understand that she is a separate individual, that other people have feelings, and that their feelings "feel" much like hers, she can start to learn the different ways of interacting with parents, siblings, grandparents, friends, and strangers. This is a complex series of behavior patterns to master, yet your child will be well on her way toward successful interaction with practically anyone by the end of her second year.

Q & A
That Bad Girl . . .

Q: Recently my twenty-month-old, Richard, has been coming home from his child-care center rambling on about "bad girls" and "blocks." I finally figured out by going there and watching that Richard's upset because a small group of older girls occasionally monopolize the block corner. The staff doesn't seem to think it's an issue that they should get involved in. They say Richard doesn't have any trouble with the other kids, that the blocks are available to him sometimes (thought not always when he'd like), and that this situation will work itself out.

I understand that the girls should be allowed to play by themselves with the blocks if they want, but on the other hand I don't like to see my child repeatedly rejected by a group at such a young age. What really worries me is the fact that I can't seem to get my son interested in finding other friends. He seems completely caught up in his desire to get those girls to let him play with them. What should I do about this?

A: It's hard not to want to rescue your toddler from an unpleasant situation with other kids, but the caregivers at your child's center may have taken the correct approach in this case. In general, your child can best explore the complex ins and outs of playing with others and making friends if the adults who care for him are watchful but not intrusive (unless, obviously, someone is about to get hurt). Interfering in such interactions as you've described harms a child's ability to learn to help himself. At your child's age, observing and interacting with older kids can be a plus, even if they aren't particularly friendly. Anyway, he's probably more focused on the blocks right now than the fact that the girls are trying to exclude him.

For all these reasons, it might be best to wait and see how the situation works out. Ask his caregivers to monitor your child's interactions with others, though, and make sure this exclusion scenario doesn't get too prolonged. Meanwhile, try to drop in occasionally at lunch or a little early at the end of the day and read a story to your child—so that he will know that he has your support—and point out and discuss interesting friends his age once in a while. Quite soon, the attraction of playing in the block corner when the older girls are there will probably fade. They may even tire of the block corner eventually and leave it all to him!

"LOOK—IT'S ME!":
SOCIAL ACHIEVEMENTS IN THE FIRST
TWO YEARS

The age at which scientists believe that infants are aware of their separate selves has been pushed back repeatedly, as methods of determining developmental advances are regularly improved. The ability to move at about six to nine months certainly provides babies with more experience of their separateness and opens up new opportunities to encounter objects and other people. Gradually, your baby transfers her focus from her own physical sensations toward these objects outside herself. (At about this time, she uses her first words to name them, further demonstrating that her attention is moving outward.)

As she proudly masters the names of one object after another, your child becomes increasingly aware of, and interested in, your responses to her actions. By now she is cognizant of the fact that her thoughts are separate from yours and that they may be very different. She will begin the process of *social referencing*—that is, looking to you after she performs an action or, if the two of you witness an event, checking your reaction to it. This is one of the first clear signs of her growing awareness of her social world.

At around eighteen months, a number of cognitive advances come together to move your child forward in her social development. Whereas she was previously instinctively attracted to videotapes of babies' faces (and to babies' faces in picture books), she now becomes aware that the faces belong to "others" who are not herself. Likewise, while she loved to look at herself in the mirror at six, nine, and twelve months of age, she now understands that she is actually looking at a reflection of herself! At twelve months, she would point at an object (and perhaps name it) even if no one else was in the room. At eighteen months, she will point out the object only if someone is there. Her developing language skills have helped her realize that she can share experiences and compare reactions with others through gestures and words.

The period between eighteen and twenty-four months is a time of deepening social relationships. With the great jump in verbal ability, your child is able to attempt more sophisticated social interactions. She becomes fascinated by others' emotions and gradually begins to realize that other people can experience the same kinds of preferences and feelings that she does. By her second birthday, she will have begun enjoying play dates, will learn a great deal by imitating other children, and may even refer to her friends by name when they're not there. Still, unless her parents encourage her to engage actively with other children, her play will remain largely parallel with theirs until well into her third year. She may sit literally back to back with her best friend as they play, even when they're doing the same thing.

THE TOY BOX
At Twenty Months

Tally's friend Theo has come for his third play date, and the two are happily pulling one toy after another out of the toy basket, as though they're competing to see who can get them out the fastest. Suddenly Theo stops, entranced by the red ball he has found at the bottom of the basket. "Ball!" he announces with satisfaction. Theo and Tally's moms, who are chatting nearby, glance at him and smile.

"That's a funny ball, Theo," Tally's mom, Ruby, says, going over to demonstrate. "Look, it makes a jingly sound when you roll it." She rolls the ball. Theo laughs when he hears the sound and runs after it. Ruby turns to smile at her daughter, but Tally has a frown on her face.

"Mine!" Tally says, getting up and racing toward the ball. She grabs it and holds it aloft just before Theo reaches it. "My ball!" she tells him sternly.

Theo reaches for the ball, starting to wail with frustration. "Theo, it's Tally's ball," his mother, Holly, says. She moves toward the toddlers as Theo's wails get louder.

Ruby can see that this situation will only get worse. The parents will have to physically separate the children, and Tally and Theo will lose their chance to practice playing together. But she has an idea. "Tally, look!" she says, reaching into the toy box for another ball. "Here's your blue ball with the sparkles! You love these sparkles, don't you?"

Gently, she manages to exchange the pretty blue ball for the red one in Tally's hands. As soon as Tally's attention is diverted to the blue ball, she drops the red one to the floor.

"Ball!" Theo says. He sits down on the floor, placing the red ball between his legs with great satisfaction. Tally sits down, too, her back to Theo, making her blue ball roll away.

Ruby and Holly exchange relieved glances. A potential problem has been avoided without the adults trying to force their children to "share" when they're not yet able. Tally and Theo are not playing together, but at least they are successfully playing side by side. Perhaps there will be a good opportunity to experience taking turns or sharing later in the play date. If not, at least the playtime will end without any practice in hitting.

"PLAY WITH ME": LEARNING TO BE WITH OTHERS

The road toward successful interaction with other human beings is a long and challenging one for any child. Your one-year-old will be grateful for all the support and social interpretation you can provide. One way you can help is to be aware of where your child is developmentally, in order to avoid demanding too much or expecting too little in her social interaction. Between twelve and fifteen months, for example, it probably isn't possible to curb your child's behavior by pointing out its effect on someone else. The fact that her hitting Sarah on the head "hurts Sarah's feelings" will certainly fascinate your child (and is important for her to hear, so that she can eventually begin to understand it), but it probably won't convince her to stop hitting Sarah. In fact, if you make too big an issue of the incident—snatching your child away, getting emotional, and otherwise giving her more and richer attention than usual—you will actually encourage the behavior by focusing her attention on it. A better response would be to model good behavior by apologizing to the other child on your child's behalf, make sure she is cared for, then separate the two of them and explaining calmly but firmly to your child why her action was wrong. (She isn't likely to understand the abstract concepts as you tell her that her behavior was "bad" or "mean," but she will learn from your tone of voice that you do not approve.) You can then put the children back together (if both are willing), remaining there yourself to make sure that they don't fight again. If you see that they're headed for another confrontation, gently guide their interaction in positive directions. In general, it's best to work on preventing such situations rather than trying to deal with them after they've occurred.

By eighteen to twenty-one months, your child has begun to perceive the fact that another person's feelings are much like her own. This can certainly help with biting and hitting issues, if you continue to monitor them calmly and consistently. However, other issues come to the fore during this period that can also cause difficulty on the playground or during play dates. These spring from your toddler's low frustration threshold and her increasing need to try to control situations. At this age, for example, you toddler is more likely to bite a child because she took away her toy, or because she hit her, or because she's tired and is losing it emotionally than just because she wants to see what happens when she bites. By repeatedly showing your child specific ways to interact with others—what to say, when to share, how to get the other person to cooperate—you ease the way toward friendship and social ability.

By the end of her second year, your child will have become more interested in the concept of "good" versus "bad" behavior. Unfortunately, she will probably be quicker to judge the behavior of others before her own; this is an age when your child is likely to protest loudly when another child behaves "badly" toward her but blithely do the same thing herself a few minutes later. This is to be expected and can be gradually remedied by continuing to consistently (but not relentlessly) discuss the good and bad behavior the two of you witness in other children and in herself. Your own example—behaving calmly and fairly as often as possible in stressful situations—will instruct her even more effectively than words. Mean-

A back-to-back position enables each child to stay focused on his or her own play, although others' play will invoke curiosity.

while, her deepening perception of the emotional world of others will lead her to express her affection for her friends more frequently, making for more pleasant and rewarding interactions.

As we have seen, forming emotional connections with other children is a long process, and social interaction is not a particularly interesting idea to your child until her second birthday or even later. Just as when in an unfamiliar city you would probably want to familiarize yourself with the layout of the area before venturing forth, your child needs to get to know herself a bit before she's ready to connect with others. At twelve months, she doesn't especially enjoy meeting strangers (though she will probably show more interest in other children than in adults). Between eighteen and twenty-one months, she is still likely to enjoy solitary or parallel play and spend a lot of time "talking" to herself in jargon or early words. By this time, though, her stranger anxiety has probably abated, and she may begin to enjoy playing with familiar adults for longer periods of time. This greater ease with adults other than parents is why, as you may notice at the child-care center, children this age tend to cluster around the caregivers rather than play with each other. In general, your child knows that the other children are there, and they are becoming more important to her, but her drive to experiment with objects and master her environment is still stronger than her desire to make friends. In other words, if your eighteen-month-old is more interested in her cousin's toys than in her cousin when he comes to visit, at least you know she's developing right on schedule.

The social situation changes dramatically, though, at the end of the second year. Finally your child is ready to begin exploring the social realm. Toddlers at this age are often quite eager to meet other children, and they begin imitating and learning from their behavior at a tremendous rate. If you have been considering putting your child in a group child-care situation, this might be a good time. A high-quality setting with a caregiver for every three or four toddlers can provide structured play that incorporates lessons in such social skills as turn-taking, sharing, and controlling negative behavior.

EASING THE WAY
Play Dates

Getting together with another parent and child is nearly always a good idea, but at first the benefits may well be more yours than your child's. As the year begins, you can watch other parents with their children, learn some new techniques, and offer some of your own insights to them. At this point, your children won't play together much at all, but they are interested in the fact that other children like themselves exist. If your child has no siblings, it's especially helpful to introduce her to children in her neighborhood. As she progresses past the middle of the year, they still won't be "friends," but they will benefit from their familiarity with one another. You and the other parent will be able to monitor their social experiments (transfer of objects, hitting, etc.) in a safe, well-controlled environment. Meanwhile, you'll be plugged in to the neighborhood grapevine, picking up information on which child-care centers, children's programs, and nursery schools various parents prefer. By the time she reaches age two and actually begins to show an interest in the idea of having a friend, she'll already have one contact. Since both of you will be familiar with the other parent's and child's temperaments and behavior habits, guiding both children through their first real lessons in social give-and-take will be easier for everyone. Later, when your child begins preschool or kindergarten, she may find she has this lifelong friend in her class.

It's important to note, though, that not every random play-date arrangement works out for the best. You may find that your child and your neighbor's child experience a fundamental incompatibility (yours may be quiet and solitary, for example, while the other child is very physical and assertive). It's also possible that your parenting style and that of the other parent clash (perhaps you believe in intervening only when necessary, while the other parent constantly "hovers"). If you really feel that these play dates won't work out, there's no harm in just admitting this to the other parent and looking for another play-date partner. Some parents prefer to develop play-date relationships with two or three different children over the course of the year, so that undue pressure is not put on one relationship and so that their children can be exposed to different behavior patterns as they learn their own style of relating to others. If one child or parent causes frequent problems during play dates but you're reluctant to give up the chance to socialize, try limiting your social interactions with that family to more public places like the park or playground.

In short, no play date is mandatory at this age, and few turn out to be perfect, but most can be informative and even fun. These days, when children are rarely just "sent outside to play," play dates may be the best early tool for beginning the socialization process.

LEARNING ABOUT GOOD AND BAD: THE SEEDS OF MORALITY

The morality of children is a hot-button topic for many parents these days, especially around those times when the media provide us with new evidence that some children seem never to have learned the difference between right and wrong. The months on either side of a child's second birthday are rife with opportunities to fear for your child's moral future, if you allow yourself to run with those emotions. There are bound to be hitting, pushing, and screaming incidents; she may step on a bug just to see what happens; she may seize a candy bar from the grocery checkout stand and refuse, red-faced and tight-lipped, to give it back. It is vital, then, to keep these incidents in developmental perspective; they are *perfectly normal* incidents for children her age. Instead of seeing them as the first "warning signs" of a sociopathic disorder (a syndrome that clearly springs from much more serious beginnings than this), treat your child's social transgressions for what they are: *opportunities* to begin showing her better, more productive ways of interacting with others.

Your child will show you that she is ready for these lessons by the increase in her ability to empathize as the year progresses. More and more over the months, your toddler will try to comfort others in distress rather than mimicking their behavior or becoming upset herself. As she nears her second birthday, she may even begin to act on her empathic feelings by bringing a toy (even one of her own) to a crying child or feeding a doll that she believes is hungry. This is your chance to encourage these positive, or *prosocial,* behaviors—praising her for her kindness and generosity, describing how much better the child (or doll) she's helped feels, and treating her in similar ways so she can experience the pleasure she's learning to provide for others. If you believe that the basis of a moral life is the Golden Rule, now is the time your child can begin to learn the value of "doing unto others as she would have them do unto her."

Though your child's capacity for empathy can be greatly encouraged now, its origins lie to a large extent in how securely her attachment to her key caregivers was established in her first year of life. From you she learned the pleasure of being loved and attended to and the behavior patterns surrounding caring for another person. As she approached her first birthday, she increasingly checked your own responses to incidents you both witnessed and noted when you reacted in empathic or nonempathic ways. In the second year, your calm, consistent parenting has given her the support she needed to lock on to others' emotions as well as her own. Now, as she experiments in a wide variety of ways with interacting with other children (positively as well as negatively), you can make the greatest impact of all by clearly explaining the consequences of her actions, stating your rules of behavior, and giving her an emotional response. (For example, "Look what you did. Can you see that that hurt Amy? That's a 'no.' " Or, just as important, "What a nice idea. Grandma loves kisses. Look how happy she is.")

When she's reached age two, your child's ability to empathize is still limited, but with your encouragement it will increase dramatically through her elementary-school years. Her ability to share, help others, and sympathize will blossom with your good example and her own increasingly confident social experiments.

A BABY'S-EYE VIEW
Poor Daddy

Ice cream, twenty-two-month-old Esther says to herself with great satisfaction, running down the sidewalk holding Daddy's hand. *Esther like banilla.* Daddy's stride is enormous, and it is difficult but fun to try to keep up. She enjoys the differences in his movement compared to Mommy's. "Stop!" she shouts proudly when they reach the corner. "Good, Esther. We stop and look both ways for cars, right?" Daddy responds. They wait for the "walk" sign, then proceed across the street. But as they step up onto the sidewalk, Daddy trips and falls!

"Ouch!" Daddy says (altering what he would have said if he were alone). He sits on the ground and inspects his knee. His pants are torn, and he has a cut. "Daddy needs a Band-Aid," he says a bit harshly, trying to clean up the small amount of blood.

Esther stares at the cut on his knee. She feels a familiar feeling well up inside her—it's a mixture of fear and sadness. Her lower lip quivers. She is going to cry!

"I hurt myself, didn't I, Esther?" Daddy says, more in his normal tone of voice. Esther looks at him. Her panicky feeling is replaced by a new feeling, a kind of sympathy. "Poor Daddy," she says. "Ouch." She puts her head two inches away from his and stares at his knee. She gives him a long hug, just like Mommy does when she gets hurt. She feels better now, so Daddy must. She pulls on his arm. "Up, Daddy," she says briskly. "Ice cream."

The two-year-old's increasing focus on how things are "supposed to be" also informs and supplements her first attempts at moral behavior. At around twenty-four months, your child may begin to insist adamantly that toys should not be broken, shirts should have all their buttons, and her hands should be clean. In one well-known study by Dr. Jerome Kagan of Harvard University, fourteen- and nineteen-month-old children were put in a playroom with a large number of toys, some of which were purposely flawed. None of the fourteen-month-olds paid any special attention to the damaged toys. The nineteen-month-olds, on the other hand, were very interested. They took those toys to their mothers, pointed out the damaged parts, stuck their fingers in the place where the animal's head had been removed, for example, and in many cases asked that the toys be fixed. This new concern for the "correctness" of things increases as children approach their second birthday. It may cause your two-year-old to object passionately to the clothes you've chosen for her that day, but it can also bring lessons in correct behavior zinging home.

At about the same time that correctness becomes an issue, the one-year-old begins to comprehend the concept of *agency*—that is, that something (some kind of "agent") caused a thing to happen. Your child will demonstrate this ability not only through her interest in toys that do something when she punches or manipulates them, but in her triumphant cries of "I did it!" and her murmured "Uh-oh," when she flips the sugar bowl upside down. It is a wonderful experience to watch your child internalize the positive aspects of this concept—to see her private smile as she completes a simple puzzle, indicating that *she* knows she's succeeded at something even though you haven't said a word. This understanding of the fact that she can cause things to happen, coupled with her desire to keep things "correct," makes for very powerful motivation toward learning positive behavior in the final months of the second year. It is yet another fundamental basis for your child's developing moral sense, a skill that, while still primitive, will soon grow by leaps and bounds.

It is really too soon to worry about such issues as whether your child fits in with children her own age or even whether she'll ever learn to share. But if you consistently feel that your child is not taking a normal interest in interacting with other people—if she is unusually withdrawn, timid, aggressive, or off-putting in ways that don't seem to be changing over time—talk to her other caregivers about how she is when you're not present. Remember, no one, not even adults, is always the same in every social situation. Often (to our chagrin), our children behave differently when we're not around. If your child's caregiver or any other adult who knows your child well shares your concerns, however, it can't hurt to discuss them with your pediatrician. In almost every case, time will tell if your child is experiencing social challenges—and in most cases, time will alleviate the problem, too. But it is never a good idea to ignore deep-seated concerns that arise from interaction with your own child.

"WE DON'T BEHAVE THAT WAY": EXPLORING PROPER LIMITS

Every parent knows that teaching a child new skills is an uneven process, with just as many regressions as breathtaking leaps forward. The second half of this year, when your child proves just as eager to experiment with the limits of acceptable behavior as she is to test everything else in her world, can prove especially difficult. Add to that the especially painful embarrassment many parents feel when their children misbehave in social ways, and you have a potent brew for discord in your life with your toddler. If you can put aside your own emotional investment in wanting always to appear "correct," though, this time can be used to help your child experiment with limiting her behavior, and learning how to interact with others in positive ways.

The first step in this process is to help your child distinguish between

Learning to express angry feelings without using aggressive behavior is a major hurdle for toddlers and parents.

angry *feelings* and aggressive *behavior*. All children feel angry now and then; at this age, your child probably feels angry several times a day. Anger can arise as a result of the natural frustrations of this point in her development, or it might be the result of such major events as a new caregiver or a new baby in the house. As with most such situations in life, acknowledging that the emotions exist rather than trying to deny or stifle them is the first step in addressing them. You can then sympathize with your child's anger, and help her express it in words, while simultaneously trying to guide and shape the ways in which that anger is expressed. It may be acceptable in your family to punch a pillow or yell in one's own room, for example, but not to punch or yell at the baby. Helping your child distinguish between her emotions and her expression of those emotions—and between good and bad forms of expression—helps her learn to channel her anger without feeling that she's a bad person for feeling that way.

Some children seem to attract more attention to their "difficult" behavior because they are larger than other children their age or because they tend to act out when others are present rather than when they're alone. If you have a larger than average child who frequently seems to be at the center of social disruption, start talking to her about how her large size affects her behavior. You may need to gently dissuade her from enthusiastically hugging other children, roughhousing with siblings, or leaping into Grandpa's lap. Tell her, for example, "Allegra's smaller than you. You need to be gentle." Then model the desired behavior yourself by showing her how to, say, roll a ball to Allegra instead of throwing it. She may continue to be too rambunctious a lot of the time, but she'll get the point eventually.

Just as you can parent more efficiently once you discover which situations are likely to cause your child to lose control, so she can begin to monitor her own stress level by learning what her limits are. If you see your child beginning to lose it on a day when she's missed her nap, point out nonjudgmentally that she must feel overwhelmed because she's tired. If she's close to two, she'll say, "Not tired!" Rather than argue, say, "Well, *I'm* tired," and offer to read her a story or start some other restful activity. If you know that she tends to become fearful in large crowds, talk to her about any upcoming group occasions and stay with her while they're in progress until you're sure she's comfortable. Debriefing her afterward—

as in, "Did you like the clown? He had a big red nose that honked loud"—will help her process the experience and prepare her for the next one. If you know that your child has difficulty sharing her toys with her friends, prepare ahead for a play date by helping her choose ten toys to place in a basket and carry into the living room (away from her other toys) for the play period. (Encourage any fledgling impulses toward sharing by saying, "Sally might like this toy," as you drop it in the basket—and try to include pairs of similar toys to keep both toddlers happy.) Keep in mind that losing control is frightening to the child; she would like to avoid it, too. Labeling the causes of her behavior and showing her how to deal with it will help her monitor her own behavior later on.

This is a good time to show your child how to *rechannel* socially maladaptive behaviors as well. If your child constantly pounds on other kids, provide her with some pounding toys during play dates or group child care. If she is a sensitive child who cries a lot, show her that words work better than tears in gaining the attention and care of others. If she refuses to mind you or acknowledge that she hears you, give her something to do by herself until she's ready to come back and be part of the group.

As your child learns to limit her negative behavior, be sure to give her plenty of examples of positive behavior to take its place. Whenever you happen to catch her doing something right, take a moment to offer her some praise. When working out better ways to deal with specific social situations (such as taking turns or dealing with teasing), acting out the situations for her with puppets or toys can supplement the example you yourself are setting ("Look. Elmo's sad that you're not sharing."). Repetition has great value at this age as well. We sometimes forget that our children don't automatically know the rules of social interaction in our culture. They need to hear, over and over until they learn it, that hurting others is not acceptable, that crying to get one's way is not appropriate, that it is not necessary to put up with someone else's hurting us, and that helping others is a highly valued trait.

Don't Push!

"I always used to have a problem with my sister-in-law, Michelle," Annette, the mother of twenty-four-month-old Liana, told me. "Michelle is the kind of mom who can never leave well enough alone with kids. She always has to intrude on their play, showing them how to play a game better or telling them 'interesting facts' when they're just trying to have fun. I've watched her do that with her own kids for years, and after I had Liana, she started right in with her. I know she means well—she probably thinks she's enhancing their experience and making them smarter. But I'm the kind of parent who likes to let kids learn on their own as much as possible, and it really bothered me whenever Michelle interfered.

"Still, I never worked up the courage to say anything about it to her. I remember when Liana was about nine months old, Michelle gave her a jack-in-the-box. Liana was happy just watching someone else turn the crank until the clown jumped up, but Michelle kept forcing her little hand to turn the crank and saying, 'See, Liana? This is how it works. You turn the crank, and that makes the latch open on the lid.' It was driving me crazy, but I was still more concerned about offending Michelle, I guess, than rescuing Liana, because I didn't say anything and just let Michelle ruin the game.

"Then, the other night, when Michelle was over with her family, the kids had gotten out a set of blocks and marbles to play with. Liana doesn't really get the concept of stacking the blocks yet so that the holes in the middle line up and a marble can run from top to bottom. She just likes stacking a few blocks by herself, without the marbles. Needless to say, Michelle had to get right down on the floor with her, saying, 'No, Liana, look, you can line the blocks up so that the marble goes through this way—see?' I kept talking to her husband like nothing was happening, but I was really seething inside. Then, all of a sudden, I heard Liana shout, '*No,* my game! Stop!'

"There was dead silence in the room for a second. But Michelle got the message. She came back and joined us grown-ups, and Liana went back to playing with her cousins her own way, looking very pleased with herself. I know that Liana was rude to her aunt, but it was so satisfying to me to hear her *express* what she felt. If she were older, she could have said, 'I'm fine, thanks,' but at her age she did the best she could to express her need for her own space. In some ways the incident really made me understand how much she's learning about how people interact and how much she can teach me—not just the other way around. It gave me a good feeling as a mom to know she can handle herself so strongly with others. We'll just have to work on finessing her manners a little better, I guess."

"LET'S BE FRIENDS": A WIDENING WORLD OF RELATIONSHIPS

A year has passed, and two-year-old Clara has grown and developed in ways Marian and Bill could hardly have imagined twelve months ago. Once again, they are having a dinner party, this time with a couple down the street whose daughter, Kenya, has visited several times before on play dates. Because Clara continues to have problems sharing her toys, Marian has discussed with her beforehand which possessions she's willing to share with Kenya tonight. They've laid out half a dozen "acceptable" playthings and put the rest of the toy box away. As they were doing so, Marian was touched by Clara's picking up a Raggedy Ann doll, saying, "Kenya's doll," and putting it in the stack of things to be played with. *Maybe Clara is starting to think of her friends' wishes after all,* Marian thought.

The dinner goes well, and the girls play happily together, falling into the rhythm established on their play dates. They jump together on Clara's little trampoline. Marian keeps one eye on them as she chats with the grown-ups, knowing that Kenya can get aggressive and that Clara will start screaming if she's pushed. By the time coffee is served, Clara and Kenya have just about worn each other out. They continue to keep busy with the toys, but their voices have become somewhat shrill and their behavior a little testy. A few minutes later, Clara suddenly appears at Marian's side. "Blankie," she says and lays her head on Marian's lap. Marian looks down at her in surprise. Did Clara just realize she'd reached her limit and figure out what to do about it? Whether or not that was Clara's intention, her ploy worked. Kenya's parents are getting to their feet, saying it's about time they got home. A few minutes later, Marian, Bill, and Clara stand at the door, waving their guests good-bye. As the door closes, Marian gives Clara a hug. The evening went so well! And part of the credit had to go to her two-year-old, who amazingly enough was able to enjoy social time with a peer, regulate her own level of stimulation, and know on some level when to call it quits.

ADVANCES
Social Achievements in the Second Year

12 MONTHS	Social "style" begins to emerge. May be friendly, reclusive, a tease, weepy
	Likes to be read to
	Sometimes enjoys turn-taking activities
	Enjoys a wider circle of people
15 MONTHS	May try to direct others' behavior
	Teases family members
	Usually plays independently but makes sure a familiar person remains nearby
18 MONTHS	Communicates emotions physically more than through words
	May have difficulty with transitions
	Begins to obey some family rules
21 MONTHS	Starts to become interested in playing with other children
	Doesn't like to share favorite toys

	May give back toy that belongs to another child
24 MONTHS	Imitates other children's behavior
	Enjoys playing with older children
	May begin to share
	Sometimes empathizes with another's emotions
	Manages transitions better but sometimes has trouble with separation

FIRST-PERSON SINGULAR

Later, your child will enjoy looking back on the notes you keep about her social life in her second year. Be sure to write down the names of her first friends here, and note what activities they liked to do together the most. If you and another family go out on an excursion, describe it briefly and include photographs. Note when you first witness your child sharing her own toy, when she first offers a toy or a kiss to a crying friend, and when she first seems aware of your own, separate feelings. Watching the ways in which her empathy and kindness grow can comfort you on days when she's feeling a little less sociable.

READER'S NOTES

_____

_____

_____

_____

_____

_____

CHAPTER 7

Predictability Helps—
My Need for Routine

Your child needs to know what the rules are and that he can depend on them.

Angela's favorite grandmother lives 150 miles away in another state and has never had a chance to see Spencer, Angela's little boy. Angela hesitated to take the trip earlier in the year, but now that Spencer is twelve months old, she feels he's ready to interact well with a new relative. Angela is so excited about the meeting that she forgets to plan important details for the trip itself. To her dismay, Spencer begins crying the moment he is put into the car seat and hardly stops until they reach her grandmother's house. He starts crying again when he is introduced to his great-grandmother, he wails when he's offered the creamed corn she cooked for him, and when it's time to put him in the portable crib Angela has placed near her bed, he screams for so long that Angela fears he will have convulsions. "He's a real handful, isn't he?" Angela's grandmother remarks grumpily the following morning, as Spencer hiccups miserably in his mother's arms. "He must take after your mother's side of the family."

Angela may not be happy with Spencer's behavior during her vacation, but at least she can console herself with the knowledge that it's quite normal for his age. One-year-olds take comfort from familiar surroundings and daily activities. To understand what they're going through when their world is suddenly altered, imagine how shaken you would feel if you'd just started a new job and discovered that your boss had been fired, your office moved, or your lunchtime changed to 5:00 P.M.

By establishing routines, sticking to them whenever possible, and providing acceptable substitutes when the usual routines are not possible, you help your one-year-old feel confident in his world; he learns to view his life as predictable and secure. Knowing that naptime will always follow lunch (even if that nap occasionally takes place in a stroller), that he cannot have a cookie if he didn't eat breakfast, and that you will sing him a song or read him a story before he drifts off to sleep will literally take a load off his mind and free up his energy for more constructive thoughts. This doesn't mean you have to be absolutely rigid about feeding times, behavioral rules, and so on. Everyone needs to learn to deal with a certain amount of unpredictability in life. But general *consistency* is a great boon to children this age. Singing familiar songs when your child must ride in the car during naptime, providing familiar toys and books when he must sleep away from home, and bringing along a snack when he will be out of the house at lunchtime are all ways to keep his routines consistent without having to be a complete slave to them yourself.

Routines would be very easy to follow if everybody stayed in the house all day and our children's needs and desires never changed. Obviously, that is not the way the world works, however. Such routines as sleeptime, mealtimes, and even toilet training are frequently disrupted by daily demands and must evolve as the child's development progresses. Trying to come up with a proper philosophy for, say, getting your child to sleep through the night on his own is made even more difficult by the mountains of conflicting advice thrown at you by friends, relatives, parenting magazines, books, on-line services, and so on—many of them not appropriate for your child at his particular stage of life. It does not make sense, for example, to impose the "just put him to bed and let him cry himself to sleep" routine on a three-month-old infant, who is not yet physiologically able to sleep through the night without a feeding. It may not even make sense at twelve months, when, as we saw in Chapter 2, a child's overwhelming urge to practice walking may cause him to wake up in the night and need to be soothed a bit on his way back to sleep. Well-timed routines can set the stage for happy, secure children who can sleep, eat, and use the bathroom on their own, but routines that ignore a child's temperament and developmental stage or a family's lifestyle are likely to fail.

In the end, only you know which routines will work with your child at any particular stage. Which routines you choose (assuming that they work reasonably well) is not as important as the fact that you have them. Your one-year-old may not always be eager to take a bath before bedtime, but in the long run it will help him learn that bath-and-then-bedtime is a normal, inevitable part of life. Meanwhile, he will look to this predictable sequence of events as a welcome landmark in what is often a confusing array of daily events. Bit by bit, routine by routine, you can thus build a secure platform from which he can "take off" toward eventual independence.

"IS IT MORNING YET?": SLEEP PATTERNS IN THE SECOND YEAR

Because of the developmental factors that control and often disrupt a young child's sleep patterns—and because of the wealth of contradictory theories about how best to handle sleeptime routines—figuring out how to get a one-year-old to sleep is one of the most challenging aspects of this stage of parenting. Certainly, a sleep routine is necessary if your child is eventually going to learn to go to bed and stay there. He will need to figure out how to let go of wakefulness without his parents present, to get himself back to sleep if he wakes in the night, and (eventually) to get up and go to the bathroom and then return to bed if he has to. The best way to reach that goal from where you are at the beginning of the first year is to (1) observe your child's developmental state; (2) decide where, when, and how he will go to sleep depending on your family's lifestyle, needs, and personal preferences; and (3) stick to your routine until you see that it is no longer getting your child to his goal, and then gradually change it.

Developmentally, your child has some good news and some bad news for you this year. The good news is that by around twelve months, he is probably physically able to sleep through the night. His sleep cycles have lengthened since infancy, and his tendency to sleep at night more than in the day has been established, to the point at which he is able to actually get a good night's sleep. The bad news is that a number of external factors can intrude to disrupt this physical ability to sleep all night. At around twelve months, when he is learning to walk, the increased physical exertion and mental stimulation that result may prevent him from falling asleep easily and may wake him up in the night. (Think of how hard it is for you to sleep when you're in the midst of an exciting or stressful period at work or at home.) At fifteen months, his body has calmed down a bit, but more than one daytime nap (or a single nap that's too long) may keep him from sleeping well at night. At eighteen months, the frustrations and emotional challenges of the toddler begin to impinge on his ability to sleep—he starts to feel a need to resist and control his routines, and he may need a comfort object to hold on to. At around twenty-four months, nightmares—and even, for a minority of toddlers, night terrors—can happen.

A PARENT'S STORY
Bumps in the Night

"I'll never forget the first time Eliza woke up screaming," Mary, her mother, told me. "She was nearly two, and we were visiting our parents' summer house. She slept in a little toddler bed in our room, and her screams jolted Bob and me bolt upright at three in the morning. She was sitting up in bed with her eyes open, crying so loudly it was as if someone was hurting her. I rushed over to her and took her in my arms, but she didn't pay any attention to me. I realized she was still asleep, even though her eyes were open, and I tried to wake her up, but I couldn't. (I found out later that it's best not to wake children from night terrors anyway, because they get disoriented if they're snapped out of sleep, and that may scare them even more.) It was so creepy, seeing her sort of 'there but not there,' in the dark room. But after a few minutes, her screams turned into whimpers, and then all of a sudden she sighed and snuggled back under the covers. It was as though nothing had ever happened.

"The next morning, she seemed perfectly fine. When I mentioned her 'bad dream,' she didn't know what I was talking about. I decided that was just as well and didn't mention it again. We had a few more nights like that over the following few months, and then they went away just as suddenly as they'd come. I talked to her pediatrician about them. She says they're not really dreams, but something called 'night terrors'—that they're not the result of anything particularly traumatic that's going on in her life. They're just something that happens to some kids at around their second birthdays, maybe because they were overstimulated during the day. They come and then they go, usually when there's some big disruption in their lives.

"The whole episode made us more aware of how abrupt changes affect her and to plan for them a little more. Now, when we travel, we always bring her night-light along. These episodes have happened only twice more since then, and they weren't quite as scary because we all understood them and could handle them better."

When deciding on (or changing) your child's sleep routine, take these developmental stages into consideration. He may not experience all of these challenges, but by observing him you can learn what obstacles to nighttime sleep do exist and work around them. If he is currently sleeping in bed with you, for example, and your long-term goal is to get him into his own room by age two, it might be best to wait until he's fifteen months old and then move him into a crib. At that point, his motor drives will have receded somewhat (reducing the need for you to be there to pat him back to sleep), and his toddler's resistance to change may not yet have kicked in. If you want his bedtime to be a reliable 8:30 P.M. by his second birthday, start reducing his naptime as soon as he's ready (between ages fifteen and eighteen months), and be sure to wake him up early in the mornings. If you want him to learn to put himself back to sleep when he wakes up at night (so you don't have to get out of bed and comfort him yourself), check to make sure he still has his security blanket, teddy bear, or other comfort object at around eighteen months, and encourage him to use it to help soothe himself.

Developmental stages have their advantages, too. During much of this year, your child will probably remain in a crib, for example, where his ability to disrupt the household at 2:00 A.M. will be somewhat limited. Take advantage of this natural tool to enforce his sleeptime routine, and don't get rid of the crib until you feel that his routine is firmly established—probably sometime after his second birthday. After eighteen months, your child's increasing ability to comfort himself means you need to comfort him yourself less and less at night. In fact, at this age it's best to let him whimper by himself for a while, since he is probably only partly awake and will fall asleep naturally if you don't intrude. At twenty-four months, he will probably begin to resist bedtime in earnest, but by then his bedtime routine should be so firmly entrenched that he will begin to realize there's no avoiding it. Verbal and cognitive abilities help at this age, too, since he can discuss with you (to some extent) his concerns about sleep, can engage in imaginary play relating to bedtime, can flip the pages of a book by night-light, and can talk himself back to sleep when he needs to. (You can also help him understand that it's sleeptime by saying as you leave the room, "I'll be back when the tape is over," or "You can come wake me up when it's light in here.")

Q & A
Making a Break for It

Q: I am a big supporter of the idea of letting a child learn to get himself back to sleep. My twenty-month-old son, Jason, has slept in a crib in his own room from birth. Increasingly over the past months, I've noticed that if I don't go in right away when he starts whimpering at night, he usually falls back asleep. However, recently he's begun climbing out of his crib in the middle of the night. He's had a couple of falls. Now I'm up half the night worrying that he's going to hurt himself—and besides, his acrobatics keep him from falling back asleep. What should I do?

A: There's not much you can do about convincing him to stay in bed. Once he has learned that he can get out of his crib, he will continue to try to escape. The only solution is to change his environment so that he can't get out or get hurt. Once your child starts consistently climbing out of the crib (not the first time he accidentally finds his way out), lower the mattress as far as it will go. Make sure there aren't any large toys or other objects he can use to boost himself over the edge. Place the crib so that one side is against the wall, and then put some kind of cushion or pad on the floor where he might land if he does find a way to climb out. Some parents lower the side of the crib so that if the child does climb out, he's less likely to hurt himself—but the trade-off, of course, is that it's easier for the toddler to make his escape. In general, for safety reasons, it's a good idea to try to keep your child in a crib until at least age two or two and a half. (Of course, having another child might mean reevaluating this timetable.) When he's in his crib, you know he's safe, and you can complete the process of teaching him his sleep routine while he has no choice but to stay in one place.

"MORE STORY!": CREATING AN EFFECTIVE SLEEP ROUTINE

Your child's evolving sleep needs are not the only factor to consider in establishing an effective routine that will both satisfy his need for predictability and move him toward the sleep pattern you want him to have. When deciding *where, when,* and *how* your one-year-old should go to sleep, it's also necessary to take into account his temperament, your needs and your family's, the realities of your lifestyle, and even the size of your home.

Where is an issue for many parents who, for a variety of reasons, prefer to keep their babies in bed with them but are afraid people outside their family will disapprove or are finding that their child's presence is preventing them from getting enough privacy or sleep. Though the "family bed" is less common in the United States than in many other countries, there are plenty of justifications and advocates for it. Keeping the baby in bed with you allows you to tend to him at night without completely disrupting your sleep, it allows for a physical closeness that many parents (especially those who must work away from home all day) greatly enjoy, and it offers perhaps the only initial solution for parents who don't have an extra bedroom for their child. As the need for nighttime feedings recedes, however, and your growing child starts to toss, turn, and perhaps even talk in his sleep, you may start to think about the long-term goal of having him sleep in his own bed, if not in his own room. Again, fifteen months of age is a good developmental "window of opportunity" for moving your child out of your bed and into his own crib (or out of your room and into his own). However, his own temperament—how much he likes to cuddle versus how much he likes to be on his own—may become an overriding factor at any age, as may your own and your partner's desires, the size of your bedroom, etc. The point is that there is no right or wrong place for your one-year-old to sleep. What's important is to take into account his needs and yours, decide on a place for him to sleep, and then be consistent about it so that he can know where "his place" is.

When a child goes to sleep can be another emotional button for parents, especially if their child tends to fall asleep at midnight and their neighbors' children are all in bed by eight. Increasingly, it seems, parents do allow their toddlers to stay up until quite late at night, probably because so many work all day and want to spend some time with their kids once they're home. On the other hand, many parents dream of the time when they'll have their evenings to themselves again, when the children have a regular bedtime and Mommy and Daddy can relax alone once they're sleeping. (They may also worry about how they'll ever get their kids used to going to bed early so they can get up in time for school.) It's up to you whether or when you decide it's time to work toward that long-term goal of an early bedtime, but whenever you do, you'll need to take your child's particular situation into consideration. Developmentally speaking, by the time your child reaches fifteen months, you can probably cut out his morning nap and begin shortening his afternoon nap, but you will still need to consider whether he is naturally a morning person or a night person, whether you still want him to stay up late at night so you can see him, and whether it's possible for him to get to sleep early, given the size of your home, if the grown-ups are still making noise and moving about. Of course, even if he's a night person, your child can still learn to go to bed at eight-thirty—he can stay quietly in bed without falling asleep right away. You can spend more time with him early in the mornings and weekends if you don't see him enough in the afternoons, and you can be quieter in a small house if he needs to get to sleep—but these elements do need to be considered when deciding on a reasonable bedtime for your child.

How your child goes to bed is yet another aspect of the bedtime routine that changes as he gets older, yet its general consistency may be the most important. Reading your child a story before bedtime, for example, can soothe him through the motor excitement of the twelfth-month period, his emotional eruptions at eighteen months, and the general resistance at twenty-four months. Whether he is still sleeping in your bed, has been moved to his own crib, or is sleeping in a room of his own, that story will signal to him that it is bedtime and that all is right with the world. It matters less, then, whether you snuggle under the covers with him after the story, put him in his crib, play recorded music, or close the door of his room and walk away. As long as the transition from one sleep routine to the other is gradual (rather than your sleeping with him one night and leaving him alone the next), the consistency of how he goes to sleep will get him through the changes.

Again, it's important to consider all your child's circumstances, not just his developmental stage, in choosing a sleep procedure. A warm bath before bedtime is a good idea at any age—but perhaps not if you get home from work late most nights and have to cook dinner for three kids before you put the baby to bed. Putting your child in his crib at a set time and leaving him to fall asleep by himself is a reasonable practice as he nears his second birthday—but not if he shares a room with siblings who may interrupt him as he's falling asleep. As we've seen, a comfort object often works well during this year—but not if your child happens to be the type who would rather throw the blankets and toys you provide. In deciding how your child should go to sleep each night, then, think about all the sleep-ritual possibilities available to you at each developmental stage— audiotapes, teddy bears, books, baths, a nighttime walk with Daddy, a stroller ride with Mom, a rock in the hammock and a special song— eliminate the ones you don't feel you or your child could live with for the next couple of years (or more), and introduce the ones that remain, bit by bit, until you've found the routine that works best.

A predictable sleep routine is not impossible, if you keep your long-term goals firmly in mind and are consistent about the rules along the way. Whether his bedtime is seven o'clock or eleven, whether his crib is in the living room or his own bedroom, he will be grateful on some level for your predictable, reliable announcement, "Time to go to bed," at the end of the day. This explicit statement will help him begin to prepare himself for his nightly separation from you, which is understandably difficult at this age. The relaxing rituals you have incorporated in his routine will comfort him as he resigns himself to sleep. He knows (since you've refused to make exceptions) that once he's in bed, you are not going to get him up again. He may protest this policy, but he knows he can rely on it. And, like all of us, a child who knows he can rely on the rules in his world finds it much easier to fall asleep.

A BABY'S-EYE VIEW
In the Wee Hours

Dark. Michael looks around the empty room. Shadows from the moonlight crisscross the wall. Somewhere a board creaks. From down the hall, he hears the refrigerator start to hum. *Mommy!* Michael looks around wildly. She isn't here. He starts to sit up, but all the dark, empty space around him scares him, and he lies back down. He starts to whimper. "Mommy," he says out loud. There's no answer, and he grows more frightened.

Gathering up his courage, Michael stands up in his crib. The feeling of empty space behind his pajama-clad back gives him the chills. "Mommy!" he cries, grabbing the rail and giving the crib a shake. He's happy to hear some noise, especially noise that he controls. "Mommy! Here!"

Still there's silence. Michael moves his foot. It knocks against something. He looks down and can make out the dark outline of his teddy bear. *Teddy!* He plops down and picks it up, holding it against his chest. Its smell is so familiar. It's so soft. He rubs the bear's ear over and over in a reassuring rhythm. His breathing gets heavier.

Sleep comes over him like a thick, wooly blanket. Michael tries to keep his eyes open, but it's impossible. He turns over on his side, still clutching his bear. *Teddy*. He falls asleep—on his own.

"NO PEAS!":
THE DEVELOPMENT OF FEEDING ROUTINES

Feeding probably ranks second only to sleep as a major issue of concern for parents of one-year-olds—largely because we fear that we may actually be starving our children if they don't eat the food we give them each day. It's important to know that for a number of reasons (which we'll explore later in this section), toddlers this age cannot be expected to stick to a traditional rounded diet, that their feeding habits and needs will change frequently during this year, that they don't need as much to eat as we often assume, and that as long as you offer your child a variety of healthy foods, his body will get the nutrition it needs. By paying attention to your child's particular eating habits, you can begin to build a predictable routine around his natural feeding schedule. This routine will eventually provide him with the confidence to experiment with new tastes, practice his self-feeding skills, and monitor his own level of hunger.

The first element to consider in creating a mealtime routine is what you give your child to eat. By his second year, he has already had some experience with solid foods, but this is an excellent time to expand his choices. After he's reached age two, a child's tastes in food are likely to remain largely limited to what he ate while he was one. So, easy as it is to stick to the same foods every day, make a point of putting a little tomato sauce on his spaghetti once in a while and letting him try plums and kiwis as well as apples. Expose him to different food textures as well as tastes. Don't be concerned if he doesn't eat most of these offerings. He doesn't have to like them all—he just needs to know them.

Within this variety of foods, provide a little something from each of the standard food groups sometime during the day—some fruit or fruit juice, some meat, egg, iron-fortified oatmeal or other cereal—and at least a pint of milk a day (if he doesn't like milk, cheese and yogurt make good substitutes). Chances are excellent that he will not eat it all, but he will ingest the food he needs to keep going. The American Academy of Pediatrics points out that according to numerous studies, very young children naturally select foods that add up to the number of calories they need each day. If given a high-calorie yogurt to eat before lunch, for example, they will select a lower-calorie lunch, and vice versa. It's best not to interfere with this wonderful self-monitoring process, but make sure that the food your child has to choose from is healthy, nourishing, and safe.

Keep in mind that one-year-olds need much less food than we adults do. A "handful of peas" wouldn't get us far, but he may manage fine on that on any given day. When structuring his eating routine, take the long view; if he is eating pretty well over the course of each week, don't worry about what he ate on Tuesday. Occasional binges are also to be expected. He *will* tire of peanut butter one of these days. Keep his pediatrician apprised of his eating habits, keep an eye on his rate of growth, provide him with choices, and then leave his eating decisions up to him.

As the year progresses, and you have a better idea of which foods your toddler likes best, you can begin to provide his favorite cereal at breakfast and be certain that something he likes is available at dinnertime. If you continue to let him make his own decisions through this second year about what to eat (from the choices you've provided), he may become more adventurous as he approaches his second birthday. Though he will check to make sure that his potatoes are mashed and buttered just the way he likes them at dinner, he may reach for some of the broccoli that everyone else in the family is enjoying. Secure in the knowledge that he can have a grilled-cheese sandwich for lunch at home tomorrow, he may be willing at least to try the stir-fried vegetables his friend's mom has served. You will have provided a "standard menu" he can rely on, in other words— the perfect platform from which he can venture forth toward new gustatory adventures.

Of course, what's on the menu is not the only concern when trying to create a mealtime structure for your child. Issues of *where, when,* and *how* are almost as important in eating routines as in sleeping, and these requirements tend to change over the course of the year. Your child's desire at twelve months to practice walking and moving may make it difficult for him to stay in a high chair. You may find it easier to feed him while he's sitting on your lap at the table or standing and facing you. He may eat better if given frequent (and shorter) small meals rather than three larger ones at this age. Finally, finger foods he can take with him on his explorations are an efficient way for him to supplement his diet. There is nothing wrong with any of these practices—and they are all more effective if you stick with one until he no longer needs it, so he will know what to expect. Try to confine feedings to the room with the high chair or dining table, though, so you can move him back to the chair or table easily when he's again able to sit still.

By fifteen months, he will probably feel comfortable in a high chair again. At this point, his focus is more on feeding himself than on moving around. Obviously, this means more of a mess for you, but these attempts at independence are very important and need to be encouraged. To help him stay as relaxed as possible about the process, continue to offer your child finger foods during meals (they're easier for him to eat and aren't as messy), prepare for the messes that will happen (by putting a plastic sheet under the high chair and perhaps feeding your child away from the dinner table if the mess greatly upsets your spouse), and praise him for his admirable attempts to drink from a cup and master the use of a spoon.

Your child's appetite may appear to take a nosedive between eighteen and twenty-one months, leading to a period of increased anxiety for many parents. It may help to keep in mind that one of the reasons for this decline is that your child is probably working hard to feed himself with cup and spoon now, and these utensils naturally transfer less food into his mouth than a bottle and his fingers used to. His increasing drive to experiment may also inspire him to treat his food as a toy; he may prefer to toss a piece of bread to the dog rather than eat it. His growing familiarity with the foods you offer may also have helped him develop some strong preferences. You can help him ingest the food he needs by reliably providing his healthy favorites, offering finger foods along with food that requires a spoon, and perhaps offering him a daily bottle or sippy cup of milk to make up for what he's not getting from a regular cup.

Because your child is both eager to feed himself and not especially good at it yet, this can be a difficult age at which to take him to a restaurant. True, he does not yet have the capability of controlling his behavior in adult ways and considers all the novel accoutrements of res-

As your toddler's ability to handle a spoon and a cup grows, meals can be a more independent, though still messy, activity.

taurant dining (salt and pepper shakers, menus, coffee creamers) tantalizing toys. He may also resent the violation of a home feeding routine that he has just begun to get to know. The public nature of his "misbehavior" in restaurants may embarrass you more than is called for (though it may help to remember that you were just as disruptive at his age, and so was everyone else in the room!). For this reason, some families choose to avoid restaurants as much as possible during this period. On the other hand, if your toddler has been going out routinely since infancy, he will be used to the restaurant routine and probably easier to take out, especially if you remember to order his meal with your drinks, and not your own entrées, and if a little public disorder doesn't bother you.

By age twenty-four months, your child will probably be very proud of his self-feeding abilities and also very quick to object if you try to help him eat or offer advice. By respecting his attempts to eat as you do and avoiding helping him too much or expecting him to display "good manners" at the table at such a young age, you can prevent the real feeding problems that some children develop as they grow.

Throughout this year, it is possible to create a predictable, supportive feeding routine that also incorporates your child's evolving needs. Whether he eats standing, sitting in his high chair, or sitting at the grown-ups' table, for example, he will know that meals always occur in the breakfast room and not all over the house. Perhaps he will learn that he can decide what he wants for breakfast each morning (since you make a point of stocking his current favorite on the bottom shelf) but that he has to eat what the rest of the family eats at dinner (though, of course, you always make sure that something he likes is included). He may grow used to the fact that breakfast means finger foods (because you're in a hurry in the mornings), but lunchtime, when he's with the sitter, is a perfect time to practice using a spoon. In other words, the nature of the routine matters less than its *consistency*—but this consistent routine must also continue to suit your particular child and family. In this as in all everyday routines, the more your toddler can predict what will happen, the more secure he will feel, and the more open you are to changing the rules when necessary, the better cared for he will be.

"He Just Won't Eat!"

In my work at Boston's Children's Hospital, I have found that an inevitable source of anxiety for parents of one-year-olds (and especially for grandparents) is feeding. Toddlers' ability to get by on what appears to be astonishingly little food sparks families' fears that they aren't caring for their children properly. If you are anxious about how little your child eats, he is likely to have picked up on your emotional state, and this could cause him to resist eating even more. In many households, this combination of a parent's anxiety and a child's resistance creates an intense power struggle that becomes an unintended part of the "mealtime routine."

You can best avoid this kind of vicious cycle by allowing your child to eat what he wants (and no more) during mealtimes, then removing him from his high chair and not giving him more food until the next meal. (Remember, though, that given your toddler's desire to move and limited attention span, four or five mini-meals work better at this age than three large ones.) Once he has realized that when he's done eating, the meal is over and that he gets to eat only during mealtimes, he'll learn to eat then. A toddler can hold out for an astonishingly long time, though, if he senses that his behavior creates a response in you, so be consistent—and stay calm. His hunger will eventually overcome his resistance.

"GO POTTY":
TOILET TRAINING

Unlike sleeping and eating routines, using the potty is a wholly elective activity rather than one that springs from a physiological need. As with other developmental accomplishments, however, there are windows of opportunity for toilet training that make the process easier for everyone at some times than at others. The best way to spot such an opportunity is to know your child. Has he become interested in the fact that you (or his big brother) use the potty? Does he seem intrigued when you read him a book about a child learning to use a potty or when you show him the new underwear you bought for him? If he seems aware that he is about to have a bowel movement—if he stands stock-still and stares at you a moment before his face turns red, runs behind the couch, or simply tells you he's about to "go"—he's certainly showing signs of readiness for toilet training. However, there's no need to push the process. Toilet training usually occurs between eighteen months and four years. Avoid starting when you're far along in a pregnancy, when there's a new sibling, or when your child has some other major change to deal with. Those issues aside, it's best to bring the subject up gently once in a while, see if your child's interested, and wait to start the process until he's clearly ready.

The end of the second year is often the time when a clear window of opportunity for toilet training (also called "toilet teaching") occurs. By that time, your child is no doubt over the excitement of learning to walk and is willing to sit down for short periods of time. He is probably verbally advanced enough to understand you when you explain that the new potty seat is his and that he can use it just as you use yours. "Mine" is often an important concept at this age, and the mere fact of having his own seat may be enough encouragement for him to begin using it. Toddlers nearing their second birthdays also love to imitate behavior, particularly that of older siblings. Many younger siblings train themselves to use the potty just so they can "be like" their brothers or sisters. This is also an age at which your little one may begin to demonstrate a sense of order. If he likes putting things away sometimes and enjoys knowing the proper places for objects, he may be ready to transfer that sense of order to his potty.

The first requirement for proper toilet training is physiological readiness. Research has shown that most children can't voluntarily control their bladder and rectum until at least eighteen months of age. Once your child has passed this milestone, you must also wait for him to show some sign of interest in or awareness of what's happening in his diaper. If he grunts and pulls at his pants while having a bowel movement, he is aware, and if he tells you what has happened, he is clearly interested in your reaction and in getting cleaned up. Finally, he must have reached the "imitative" stage and not currently be in one of the resistant, negative stages that are so common for toddlers. Trying to toilet-train your child

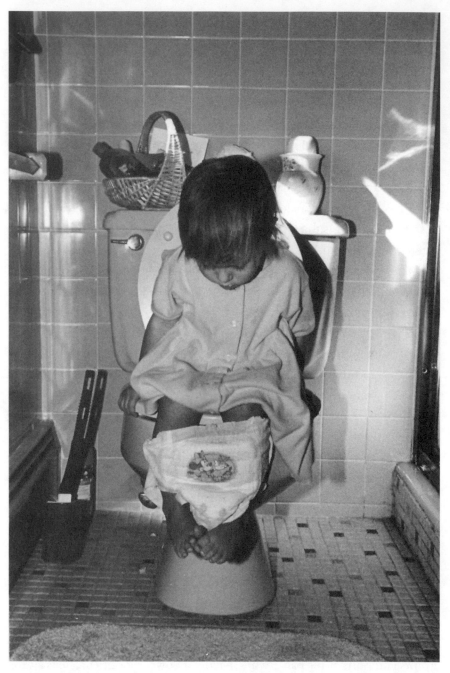

Later in the second year is a good time to introduce concepts such as sitting on the potty, although toilet training success is no doubt far away.

when he is in the midst of a "No!" stage will not only doom you to failure but may cause such reactions as his withholding his stool altogether, which can lead to painful constipation.

Once your child has entered a relatively tidy, compliant, and imitative developmental stage, however, he is ready for a first attempt at learning to use the potty. (If this attempt is not successful, don't worry—there will be plenty of other opportunities later on.) You might begin by getting one of the many children's books dealing with this issue and reading it a number of times to your child. Point out the potty pictured in the book, and talk about how all children learn to use one eventually. If your child knows older children who uses the toilet, remind him of this fact. (With his concrete toddler mind, it's much better if he can actually see another child complete the process.) Speak admiringly of that child's underwear (or the underwear of the child in the potty-training book), and then buy some for your child. Place a potty in the bathroom near your toilet, and talk about how soon your child will be "big" and able to use the potty and wear underwear just like the other big kids. In the interests of keeping the process as simple as possible, boys should be taught to urinate sitting down. This way, they will be in place to defecate as well. After your boy has learned to use the toilet consistently, he can move on to urinating while standing.

Don't expect all of these ideas to take hold right away. Keep in mind that using the toilet is not a simple development; it involves a number of new concepts that your child will need time to ponder. Meanwhile, if he signals that he is on the verge of having a bowel movement, offer to help him do it on the potty. He will probably refuse, but the connection will gradually be made for him. Allowing him to wear his new underwear at home sometimes, rather than a diaper (or letting him run around without anything on his bottom), may speed the process, since it will be easier to get him undressed and sitting on the potty in time to use it.

When he first succeeds at using the potty, praise him sincerely but not overwhelmingly. (Then he won't feel too bad when the next, inevitable accident happens.) Proudly tell the rest of the family about it later that day, and let them praise him, too. The more he feels that he is being initiated into the world of "big people," the more effort he is likely to make in completing the training process. Your continued example, the stories about successful potty-using you keep telling him, and his pride in his new, diaperless state will greatly motivate him.

Toilet training is not a smooth process, however, and there are bound to be a number of rough spots. When your child has an accident on the floor, wets his pants, or loses interest in the potty, be careful not to scold him about it. Getting upset will only make the training process unappealing, and he may stop trying. Though it doesn't hurt to remind him exactly what he's supposed to do when he senses he needs to use the potty (he may actually have forgotten) and to reiterate the positive effects of potty-using, criticizing him or losing your temper over a mess can only prove damaging. Be upbeat (as in, "Oh, well, you'll get to the potty next time. Can you get a new pair of underwear from the bureau, please?"). If he continues to have accidents, there is no shame in reverting to a diaper for a time (and he will probably not mind). Now that you have created a *routine* for using the potty, he will be able to make use of it whenever he decides he's ready.

Child-development experts generally agree that the second year is usually not the time to achieve toilet-training success, but it is a time when *preparation* for training can take place. (For ideas on how to prepare, from such experts as Dr. T. Berry Brazelton and toilet-training specialist Ann Stadtler, visit the "Toilet Training 101" site on-line at www.totalbabycare.com.) Ideally, your child will have plenty of time to get used to the idea before he has to put it into practice. As he grows older, preschool requirements may place pressure on him to accomplish this task, but at least the presence of other toilet-trained children will encourage him to follow suit. It is useful to keep in mind the fact that girls often complete toilet training at an earlier age than boys. Even twin siblings may feel ready to go through the process at entirely different times. This just goes to show that of all the routines explored in this chapter, the toilet-training process must remain the most child-driven. Attempts to direct a child's progress when he isn't ready for toilet training simply do not work for you or your child.

ON THE ROAD:
MAINTAINING ROUTINES WHILE
TRAVELING

Family vacations and out-of-town travel can provide fascinating stimulation for your child, but they can also destroy the well-established routines on which he has just begun to depend. In order to ensure a happier trip for everyone, it pays to think ahead about the ways you can incorporate your child's usual schedule into your temporary life on the road. You can begin by familiarizing your child with your travel destination as much as possible. If you're going to visit a relative or friend, call ahead of time and encourage your child to talk (or listen) to that person on the phone. Show him pictures of the people or places you plan to see. Talk about the plane, car, bus, or train trip, and read him books about other children traveling that same way.

Once you've started on your journey, your goal should be to replicate your child's home and normal routine as much as possible. Take along his favorite food in a separate bag, and try to feed it to him at the usual times. Bringing some of his audiotapes and playing them in the car can comfort him as he starts to fall asleep. Whatever you do, don't forget his "blankie," pacifier, or other comfort object and some of his favorite books and toys! Finally try to allow him something like the amount or kind of movement he's used to as well. If you are traveling by plane, take him for a little walk through the airport and down the airplane aisle if you can, to satisfy his urgent need to explore. If it's naptime, try to arrange for him to sleep a bit, wherever you are (or schedule plane trips at times other than naptime). If you're in a car, take frequent breaks to let him run around. Continue to talk to him about where you're going and when you plan to return home. He won't understand a good deal of what you tell him (and there will inevitably be some settling on both ends of the trip), but your reassuring tone and constant presence will comfort him.

THE TOY BOX
At Twenty-two Months

Charlie is upset. Without much warning, he was put onto an airplane with Mommy and flown to a place called Florida. The flight schedule prevented him from taking his nap on time, he didn't like the food the flight attendant gave him (he'd already eaten the treat that Mommy brought when they were in the airport), and now Mommy's unpacking their suitcase in a strange hotel room. Charlie looks around the room. *Nothing* here looks familiar! All the colors, angles, smells, and sounds are wrong. Feeling completely out of kilter, he starts to wail. But just then Mommy pulls out a bag that he recognizes—it's the bag he uses to carry his things to the child-care center. "Look, Charlie, your toys came to Florida, too," Mommy says. She opens the bag, and out spill Charlie's stuffed giraffe, his dump truck, his toy xylophone, and his favorite blocks. Charlie's body immediately relaxes. He is filled with relief. "Charlie's toys!" he says, plumping down on the floor beside them. He picks up the turtle and hugs it. Who cares where they are? His toys still make him feel better.

GETTING READY FOR CHANGE: THE ADVANTAGES OF GROUP ACTIVITIES

As your child nears the end of his second year, he will have gained confidence and a sense of security through his reliance on the routine you have created together. Soon he will be ready to turn outward toward those outside his immediate family and meld their attitudes, habits, and routines with his own. Eventually, entry into preschool, kindergarten, or elementary school will require him to move out of the routines of home life and into the established routines of group activity. (For children in group care, of course, this happens even earlier.) To begin to prepare your child for these experiences, you might consider partaking in a group activity this year, such as a weekly story hour at the library, an early-childhood music program, or even a gymnastics or swim class for toddlers.

It is fascinating for a growing one-year-old to realize that other routines exist besides the ones established in his own home and to watch another adult besides his parents take charge of a group of kids. Learning new activities (swimming, singing songs and dancing, jumping on a small trampoline) and incorporating group routines that include greeting a teacher, interacting with other children and their parents, and saying good-bye introduce your child to a wider world of structure and proper behavior. As he participates in these activities, he will gradually begin to realize that other children behave differently or have different "customs" and backgrounds from the ones he knows. Discovering that "Janie hits," "Rose can swing on the rope," or "Eleni likes to dance with her mommy" holds a fascination for the toddler. They also open up ways to talk with your child about how *you* do things, and why. In general, the more your child is able to understand and rely on her own family routines, the greater his ability to tolerate others' is likely to be. As you and your child get to know more and more people together in the coming years, you will be glad you took the time to establish what is "our family way" so that others' ways will prove less threatening and more interesting to compare.

EASING THE WAY
When Routines Differ

These days, it doesn't make sense to assume that a young child lives in only one home with only one "normal routine." If you and your child's other parent live apart or if your child spends a great deal of time with a relative or other caregiver, he may be growing up with two very different sets of daily routines. Problems can arise when these routines conflict or when the adults involved remain unaware of how the other conducts the one-year-old's day. Mom may serve dinner at home every evening, for example, while Dad takes his toddler out to eat on his night with him. A child's parents may not mind if he doesn't eat all his dinner, while the grandparents who care for him when his parents are out of town cannot tolerate his leaving food on his plate. Frequently a caregiver will have a hard time getting a child to go to bed because she hasn't been told, for example, that he wants his story *before* his bath instead of after. Clearly, the parents' first step in helping their child adjust to a switch between routines is to communicate to the other caregiver what their own routines have been. If your child needs a pacifier to lull himself to sleep at home, by all means tell the other caregiver this before he or she takes charge. Routines and rules involving television, bedtime, meals, and so on should be discussed among all adults concerned—and compromises arrived at in cases where the adults cannot make their routines consistent.

Try to involve your child as much as possible in the process of negotiating the new routines. As young as he is, he will feel better if *he* "agrees" ahead of time that he doesn't have to watch a children's videotape before naptime at Dad's house but can listen to an audiotape instead. (He may still protest, but at least he won't have been taken by surprise.) If he is not allowed to leave food on his plate at his grandparents' house, maybe he'll feel better about it if you ask them to let *him* decide how much he wants put on his plate in the first place. Keep in mind that while it's nice for routines to be consistent from house to house or caregiver to caregiver, young children are very adaptable and learn a lot from encountering new sets of rules and adult attitudes. In the end, the most important issue for your child is his emotional environment. As long as he understands that the adult in charge cares for him and is doing what he or she believes is best, a change in his routine is not likely to do any harm.

"HI, GRANDMA!":
LEARNING TO ENJOY NOVELTY

It has been a long year, and Angela's embarrassment over her last visit to Grandmother's house has faded into the past. Spencer's second birthday is now approaching, and Angela is eager to repeat the visit more successfully. This time, though, Angela is more sensitive to the fact that travel is difficult for Spencer, at least at this age. He doesn't like to leave his beloved toys, his room, and the rest of the life he knows so well.

To help ensure that the trip turns out to be enjoyable for everyone, Angela started talking to Spencer about it a couple of weeks before they left home. She told some of his favorite stories about his great-grandmother (stories he'd heard a number of times before) and even called her so the two of them could "talk" on the phone. One day she got out her old photograph albums and showed him pictures of her grandmother and her big old house. To Angela's delight, he seemed particularly excited about the old swing set in the yard.

When it was time to pack, Angela asked Spencer to help her pack a few of his favorite toys. She asked for his input on what snacks to bring in the car. They brought along his favorite tapes to sing along to while she drove. Spencer still threw a fit when she had to actually buckle him into his car seat, but once she'd handed him his Baggie full of Gummi Bears and popped the first tape into the player, he was fine again.

This time the trip took nearly twice as long, because Angela and Spencer stopped so many times along the way. When they finally arrived at Grandma's house, they were both tired and cranky. Once again, when Angela lifted Spencer out of the car and held him up to her grandmother to hug, Spencer burst into tears. But this time, instead of apologizing and feeling embarrassed, Angela comforted Spencer and got out his wind-up musical bear. Then she chatted with Grandma for a few minutes, giving Spencer some time to settle down. Soon Spencer's tears were dry, and Angela's grandmother was actually smiling at the way he cuddled his bear close and stared in wonder at the old swing set. "Come on, Spencer," she said, leading the way. "I'll show you the slide."

ADVANCES

How the Need for Routine Evolves in the Second Year

12 MONTHS	May self-comfort with a security object in strange places

	Appreciates storytime
	May notice when familiar people are missing
18 MONTHS	Needs time to adapt to new situations
	Obeys simple rules
	Develops clothes preferences
	Bedtime routine helps reduce nighttime fears
24 MONTHS	Enjoys family routine
	Major changes (a new sibling, etc.) may trigger regression

FIRST-PERSON SINGULAR

Your child's routines evolve so quickly—while his need for them remains so strong—that you may temporarily forget he will not *always* have to have the blankets pulled over him, then back off, before he can go to sleep at night. Before you forget about them, record his quirky routines on this page. Note when he stops needing a particular comforting routine, and try to figure out why. Record the ways in which routines helped you get through a challenging period, so that you can benefit from your experience with your next child or prepare for later challenges with this one.

READER'S NOTES

_____

_____

_____

_____

_____

_____

_____

_____

_____

_____

_____

_____

_____

_____

_____

_____

_____

_____

CHAPTER 8

Drawing the Line—My Need for Limits

Distraction is a terrific way to avoid unnecessary conflict.

What a morning! The alarm didn't go off, and both Fred and his wife, Linda, are late for work. They rush about the house, pulling on sweaters and searching for shoes. At first, neither of them notices twelve-month-old Emily amid the chaos, toddling into the bathroom with a toy clutched to her chest. She moves closer to the toilet, stops, and slowly lifts the toy over the bowl.

Fred, hurrying past the doorway, sees what she's up to. "Don't throw that in there!" he says, stopping in his tracks. Emily looks up at him, but the hand holding the toy continues its downward curve toward the toilet. "I said don't!" Fred shouts, taking a step toward her. The toy drops into the water.

"Emily, I said no!" Fred yells. Emily looks up at him, then down at the toy, and bursts into tears. Fred hesitates, not knowing what to do. Should he comfort Emily? Spank her? Give her a time-out? Should he blame her for disobeying him, or was this his fault for not having distracted her in time? Finally he picks her up. "That's okay," he mumbles guiltily. But then he thinks, *Why am I apologizing?* She's *the one who dropped the toy.*

Discipline is one of the most difficult aspects of parenting for many adults. Setting limits and enforcing rules makes us feel guilty ("I hate being the bad guy"), particularly if we remember some excessive discipline experiences from our own childhood or if we confuse discipline with punishment. Besides, with both parents often at work all day, we long to come home to a happy, smoothly running family. But, as I've pointed out before, young children tend to save their most provocative behavior until their parents get home in order to try it out in a safe environment. Sometimes we feel as though the "nicer" we are to our kids, the more meltdowns we suffer at home. Facing a relentlessly active toddler, we find ourselves struggling with our tempers and wondering what we're doing wrong.

In fact, children—even one-year-olds—need more than niceness from their parents. Perhaps more than any age group, toddlers require boundaries, rules, and a reliable structure to help them find their way in an often confusing world. Discipline means setting limits—not just taking away a toy when it has been misused but also monitoring with your child how much stimulation she can handle and encouraging and reinforcing positive behaviors. This chapter will explore ways in which you can begin helping your one-year-old learn to control her own behavior, making it possible for the entire family to live under one roof more peacefully. By thinking now about the limits you want to set for your child, in the context of her temperament and its unique challenges, you will begin to give her an idea of what is expected of her and help her continue to grow in a safe, supportive environment.

EASING THE WAY
Trying to Be a Big Girl

Many of your child's behavioral difficulties during this year are likely to stem from the gap between her desire to do things herself and her ability to do them. In trying to put on her pajamas, she may become frustrated, and her inability to verbalize her frustration may increase her anger even more. In such a situation, she's quite likely to throw the pajamas aside, refusing to get ready for bed. Instead of focusing on her "misbehavior," try helping her verbalize her frustration and then talking her gently back through the process of getting dressed. Giving her words to express her feelings ("It's hard to find the sleeve") helps her to calm down, and helping her take care of herself demonstrates to her that she will learn to do so without your help one of these days. Next time you might start to help her (as unobtrusively as possible) before she loses emotional control. In general, staying one step ahead of your child, helping her not get stuck, is one of the best ways to avoid unnecessary conflicts.

"MORE, MORE!": LEARNING ABOUT LIMITS

Discipline—or the setting of limits—begins in infancy, although we don't generally see it that way. From birth onward, a baby's actions are molded by her parents' responses. Gradually she learns to predict the consequences of various behaviors. She may observe, for example, that a smile generates a happy response, while an angry yell inspires a frown or sudden absence of physical contact. Over the ensuing months, social interaction, sleep habits, feeding patterns, and other activities will all be affected by the consequences they tend to generate. In general, though, the more common idea of "discipline"—that is, the conscious teaching of appropriate behavior—does not become much of an issue until around the first birthday. At this point, when your child is becoming much more mobile and is able (and seemingly eager) to get into one dangerous situation after another, it becomes necessary to introduce clear, specific limits to her behavior. She will need to learn to respond to a clearly expressed "No," before she's able to decide for herself whether her behavior is appropriate or not.

Fortunately, at just about the time your child is learning to walk, she becomes very interested in testing your responses to her actions. When she totters over to the radiator or to a forbidden kitchen cabinet and looks around to be sure you're watching her, she's checking to see whether this really is a no-no. Such actions demonstrate that she has figured out that there are acceptable and unacceptable forms of behavior. She is fascinated (if still often mystified) by these boundaries. Her constant repetition of an action that causes you to say "No" is not a sign of naughtiness at this age but a healthy signal that she is focused on learning precisely what her limits are.

If laying out the boundaries for your child were the only hurdle to master, parenting would certainly be simpler. However, a number of developmental issues complicate this cut-and-dried process of setting limits. Some of these are *physiological:* A one-year-old may hear you tell her to stop a physical action (such as throwing a toy into the toilet) but actually be unable to stop the movement of her arm once it's in progress. Some of the issues are *cognitive:* Your child may not yet have developed sufficient experience of cause and effect or sequence to understand that pulling the cat's tail *always* means that the cat will scratch her or that climbing up on the table will *always* make you mad. *Emotional* issues also can come into play: If your child feels that the best way to capture your attention is to misbehave, she will misbehave more and more frequently. It is vital to consider all of these issues when monitoring your child's actions, to ensure that you are not expecting too much in the way of good behavior at any particular stage. Sadly, children this age are physically abused more than virtually any other age group, largely because parents forget to take into account their natural limitations, and confuse verbal ability with true understanding.

As your child begins to move about her world with greater ease, she begins also to develop her own agenda that is separate from and frequently in conflict with yours. Certainly, by fifteen months, she has begun to focus on acquiring as much freedom as possible to explore. When she feels that this goal is being frustrated, she can create a substantial fuss. Parental tactics that work with older children, such as trying to reason with her or making long-term promises ("Sit still until dinner's finished, and then we'll go out for an ice cream cone"), are useless now, when your child cannot yet fully comprehend sequences or think very far ahead. The trick, instead, is to work at combining her agenda with yours as much as possible, arranging her world so that she usually wants what happens to be best for her, thus giving her frequent positive "cooperating" experiences. By allowing her to leave the table when she's finished eating, for example, or letting her eat before the rest of the family, you avoid a conflict that will get the two of you nowhere.

In the end, of course, our goal as parents is to help our children learn to discipline themselves as much as possible. By setting a positive pattern now—allowing your child to experience the pleasure of ensuring her own safety, of eating healthy foods, of "using words" instead of screaming or crying, and of behaving fairly with her peers—you can help her begin to take pride in her ability to set her own behavioral limits. She will move from what psychologists call *situational compliance* (behaving properly in a specific situation because she's been told to) to *committed compliance* (internalizing general rules of behavior because it makes her feel good to behave). As she grows ever more independent in the coming years, you will thank yourself a thousand times for having made the extra effort to help her learn to "monitor" herself from the beginning—by helping her identify what sets her off (feeling hungry, perhaps, or tired), exploring different coping strategies with her (such as getting out a book to look at when she's overstimulated and needs to settle down), showing her how to talk about her feelings so she doesn't simply blow up, and helping her learn to ask for help early when she feels frustrated or angry.

A PARENT'S STORY
Choosing the Rules

"When my son, Raul, and I started getting together with other kids and parents for play dates, I realized that my rules for Raul were a lot stricter than those the other parents had," Maria, a former colleague of mine, told me. "I never let Raul watch any television, and he wasn't allowed to eat junk food. When the other moms found that out, they acted like I was over the top. Their comments made me start to wonder about myself as a parent, and pretty soon I started to make exceptions. I let Raul eat at a hamburger chain a couple of times, and, of course, after that he had a fit when I didn't want to take him there again. After I let him watch children's TV a couple of times, he acted like he was addicted to it. I thought I might have to get rid of the television completely just to make him leave it alone.

"After a while, I decided that being wishy-washy about the

rules was worse for Raul than any of my rules would be, as long as I stuck to them. I thought about the reasons I'd come up with those rules in the first place, and I realized that I still believed in them no matter what anyone else said. So I decided to stand by them after all, at least when we were at home or out on our own. After a while, Raul's behavior cleared up a lot. I think he likes knowing what's allowed and not allowed. I learned that being consistent is easier on both of us, and he's learning that hamburgers and french fries aren't the most important thing in the world.

"THANK YOU FOR SHARING": EFFECTIVE WAYS TO SET LIMITS

One reason discipline becomes such a difficult issue is that many parents assume that a one-year-old behaves well in order to please them and misbehaves in order to provoke. In fact, though, your responses to her behavior are not as important to your one-year-old (at least in the first half of this year) as is the overpowering urge to explore. When the opportunity arises to taste the dog's food, her very real need to experiment with what is right in front of her will probably win out over any dimly perceived notion that you might disapprove. Looked at in this way, it's hard to get angry at your child for such an action; she's only following her natural instincts. During this period, when her developmental urges can get her into so much hot water, it's best for everyone to plan ahead for the inevitable by keeping the dog food and any other very troublesome temptations out of her reach. Gradually, you can reintroduce these items as she becomes better able to monitor her own behavior.

Distraction is a terrific way to avoid unnecessary conflict, and one that is often undervalued during this period. Parents may feel that simply changing their one-year-old's activity when she has done something wrong does not teach her anything, overlooking the fact that there are times when a child is simply not cognitively or emotionally prepared to learn about a particular issue at a particular time. It is extremely difficult for a one-year-old to take turns, for example. If your child refuses to give another toddler access to a game or toy, distracting her with a different toy while the other child takes a turn with the first one solves the immediate problem without tears or a scene. Of course, distraction doesn't teach her to take turns, but it allows her to continue interacting at a time when she's not really ready to learn that lesson.

Meanwhile, it's important to show her how she *should* behave, by praising her good behavior as it randomly happens. If your child happens to let another child play with her doll during a play date, thank her for sharing and tell her that "Mommy's proud you shared." If she tells you that a child has hit her (instead of just hitting the child back), tell her how much you admire her ability to "use her words," and then help her solve the conflict. Inevitably, on another occasion, she will refuse to share or will hit another child, but her awareness of what constitutes *good* behavior will increasingly help to curb those impulses as her ability to control her behavior expands.

Because one-year-olds' ability to reason is so limited and their desire to "behave" so sporadic, parents often (understandably) fall back on that tried-and-true behavior modification tool, the bribe. Telling your child she can have a cookie if she eats all her carrots may work very efficiently today. The problem is, you may have to offer her a cookie next time you want her to eat her carrots, too. In the long run, such a reward may even lessen her interest in the related behavior (if she's not in the mood for a cookie, there's no way she will eat those carrots). For this reason, it's best to use such external rewards sparingly and to keep them as minimal as possible. Rewards (such as gold-star stickers displayed on a poster at around age two) can be effective in "hooking" your child on a new means of doing something, but they should not be expected to have a strong or lasting effect without other positive reinforcement.

One of the best ways to guide your child's behavior over the long term is one that is frequently forgotten or ignored by parents—the power of modeling good behavior yourself. Very young children specialize in imitation. They are uncannily observant and learn a great deal from what they see. If you are in any doubt about this, look around at your friends' children. Is their walk similar to their parents'? Do they have a similar sense of humor? The same way of interacting with others? The same serious, fearful, aggressive, or playful approach to life? Quite frequently, children pick up habits from their family members—and social behavior is no exception. The best way to ensure that your child will share with others, then, may be to share with her (and with others) yourself. If you want her to speak to others with respect, make sure you do so as well. In this context, it's a particularly ironic and unproductive parenting technique to spank a child because she bit or hit or otherwise acted aggressively.

THE TOY BOX
At Twenty-four Months

It's early morning. Joanna has hopped out of bed and wandered into the living room, eager to play with her new sticker book and stickers, but she hasn't had breakfast yet. "You can play with them after you eat your oatmeal," Mom says. Joanna protests loudly, but she knows from experience that Mommy doesn't relent in these matters, and soon she reluctantly gives up her stickers in favor of the oatmeal. After breakfast is over, Mommy hands over the sticker book. "Good for you," she says. "You ate all your oatmeal! Now you're ready to start your day. Do you want me to play with you?"

Smiling, Joanna opens the book and, with her mother's help, happily places a sticker on the first page. She registers the connection between the pleasure of play, Mommy's positive reaction, and the fact that she finished her breakfast. Cooperating feels good, she realizes—and she's no longer hungry.

"OR ELSE!":
CREATING EFFECTIVE CONSEQUENCES
FOR BAD BEHAVIOR

Over the years, many parents have told me with great sincerity, "I never spank my child when I'm angry." As I often point out to them, it's hard to separate the emotion of anger from the action of spanking when you really think about it. Look back on the times (if any) when you were spanked as a child. You probably remember one or two spankings very clearly—how scared, angry, or sad you were, how huge and powerful your parent seemed. Now think again. Do you remember what you did to deserve the spanking? Probably not, at least in the early years of your life. The fact is that physical punishment works *against* the parent's interests in that it models the very sorts of aggressive behavior the parent is often trying to prevent and distracts from the original behavior issue. The child stops thinking about what she did wrong and focuses only on the scary and painful experience of being spanked.

For decades, Dr. Murray Straus and his colleagues at the University of New Hampshire have studied physical punishment and its consequences for growing children. They and other leading experts, including Kenneth Dodge at Vanderbilt University, have demonstrated beyond dispute that repeated physical punishment (and even the threat of physical punishment) actually increases children's aggressiveness. Spanking your child may get her to comply with your wishes at that particular moment, but it is likely to discourage her from cooperating with you in the long run. Furthermore, frequent or severe physical punishment such as hard spanking, slapping, and constant verbal abuse affects children's cognitive development. (Just as positive experiences stimulate growth in the brain, so can negative experiences stunt it.) As they grow older, children who have been routinely exposed to negative experiences tend to interpret many situations as hostile toward them when they are not. If such a child is pushed while standing in line for the slide at the playground, for example, she might assume the worst and push back or start yelling, while another child might not like being pushed but wouldn't exaggerate the situation. Clearly, physical punishment is not the answer for your one-year-old. In fact, the more you keep scary, negative emotions and behavior out of the equation, the more productive an enforcement of limits is likely to be.

Of course, it's easier to talk about remaining calm when dealing with a mischievous toddler than it is actually to do so. No matter how serene and "positive" you try to be in encouraging your child to behave well, there will be times when she shocks you with her actions. Biting another child (especially a baby) or poking Daddy in the eye may strike you as alarmingly aggressive, though both are quite normal (if regrettable) exploratory behaviors in this year. Children must try out all sorts of actions, in the same way they need to try out both good and bad feelings. If you overreact to her aggressiveness or other negative behavior during this experimental phase, you may actually end up reinforcing it. Your angry outbursts hold the same scary fascination for your little one as a car wreck on the highway does for adults, and she may be tempted to "test" your anger some more. Refusing to give her extra attention when she behaves badly is the best way to get her to lose interest in the behavior and to stop. Many a father has found that simply clearing his throat warningly can stop a toddler in her tracks—at least long enough for him to explain what the problem is. Against a generally calm emotional background, a slightly sharper tone of voice may correct your child's behavior without tempting her to explore your disapproval further.

Naturally, there are some situations in which you must immediately and forcefully discipline your child, particularly when you are trying to teach her to avoid a specific danger, such as running into the street, playing unsupervised near a swimming pool, or reaching up to touch the stove. Keep in mind, though, that punishment is more effective if it happens rarely. Save it for the really important, safety-threatening times. As with other aspects of parenting, it's best to think ahead of time about how you will enforce limits with your child, so that you're ready with a plan when the situation arises. Do you intend to use time-outs with your child as she grows older? You might as well start with that method now. When she's this age, you may have to sit down *with* your little one— but as long as she understands that she's been taken out of the action until her behavior improves, the time-out will be effective. Withdrawal of a treat is another discipline method that works well at this age and continues to be effective later on. In general, discipline seems to be most effective if it is a more or less natural result of the inappropriate behavior. For example, biting a child (if this is a frequent problem and not a first offense) may mean the abrupt end of a play date; refusal to allow her shoes to be put on may lead to not being able to go outside and play. When deciding on a form of discipline, think about your own needs as well as your child's. A time-out may give you the chance *you* need to calm down, and the physical separation may prevent you from giving in to the truly harmful urge to shake or spank her.

Whatever enforcement method you use, explain calmly to your one-year-old what you are doing and why, and keep the incident brief and low-key. (A five-minute time-out seems like three hours to a one-year-old.) She probably won't understand much of your explanation, but she will appreciate the concern and support she hears in your voice when you explain (preferably before and briefly after the time-out) why it is necessary, and she will understand on some level (despite her cries) that you are acting in her own best interests. Once the act of discipline is over, go on to other things and forget about it. By not dramatizing the incident, you allow your child to ponder the simple cause-and-effect relationship of bad behavior's leading to unpleasant results, rather than focusing on your emotional response to her action. (This cause-and-effect association is strengthened if you respond to her inappropriate action immediately after it happens.) No matter how effective your response to her behavior seems to be at the time it takes place, don't be surprised if you have to repeat the process a number of times. If she's very young, she might have forgotten the previous experience. If she's a little older, she may be "testing you" to see whether you really meant what you said. Again, this is a natural part of being a one-year-old, and it doesn't mean she's deliberately defying or ignoring you.

A BABY'S-EYE VIEW
That's a No-no!

Suzie is playing ball outside with her caregiver, Monique. The ball rolls out into the street. *Get it!* Suzie thinks, and she toddles into the street after it. "Suzie!" Monique calls, running to pull her (and the ball) out of harm's way.

The action causes Suzie to realize what she has done. *Car!* She looks up and sees an SUV speed by the place where she was just standing. Monique's face looks scared! Suzie starts to cry.

Then she feels Monique's comforting arms around her. "You're okay, Suzie. I know you forgot," Monique's voice murmurs in her ear. "But listen," the voice continues in a much firmer tone. "You must *never, never* run out into the street like that again. That is a *no*. You could get hit by a car. Okay? Don't do that again."

Suzie pulls away from Monique and swipes at her tears with her sleeve. She feels less panicky now that Monique has held her. She is able to think about what she did instead of just feeling scared. She has heard the strict tone in Monique's voice. *I shouldn't have gone there,* she realizes. She frowns and shakes her finger at the street. "Bad car!" she says.

"NO MEANS NO": CONSISTENCY COUNTS

Keeping behavioral rules simple for your one-year-old also means keeping them consistent. Smiling and saying, "Oh, how cute," when your little one twists her daddy's nose and then punishing her for doing the same thing to a child her age isn't fair to a toddler who is not yet able to distinguish between the separate circumstances. As with her daily routine, consistent and predictable limits on behavior foster a sense of well-being for a child and free up her energy for more productive pursuits. For this reason, it is a good idea to think ahead about which behaviors you feel violate your bottom line and which you're willing to let slide for now. The clearer you can be with yourself and your child about these boundaries, the easier your discipline decisions will be this year, and the less need you will probably have to enforce them. You may decide, for example, that actions that threaten your child's or others' safety are clear-cut reasons for disciplinary action (hitting a child with a toy will lead to immediate removal from the play area), but childish behaviors in adult environments can be ignored (being a nuisance in a restaurant). Your confidence in your choices is at least as important as the actual choices you make, since your child will sense any indecisiveness in your response and repeat the questionable action frequently just to watch you respond differently each time.

It helps if your decisions spring from clear, simple principles your child can begin to understand. That way, she will be able to generalize your rules more efficiently (not hitting a child with her hand as well as not hitting him with a toy) and adjust her behavior more easily as your rules change (moving from holding your hand every time she crosses the street to stopping, looking both ways, and moving on alone when she's older). By talking to her about these principles and sticking to them consistently, you can help your child begin to internalize your code of behavior, rather than simply respond to arbitrary commands.

Once you feel that you have a clear idea of what constitutes unacceptable behavior for your one-year-old, it's vital to make sure your disciplinary practices are consistent with those of the other adults in her life. Talk with and observe your partner's, caregiver's, and other involved adults' approach to discipline, and if there are disagreements, talk about them when your child is not in the room. Agreeing on general principles of behavior and how they will be enforced is not a onetime action for parents and other caregivers. You will have to have these discussions again and again as your child grows. Just keep in mind that the more you maintain a united front in matters of enforcing limits, the easier it will be for your child to know what's expected of her. In any case, it is usually not a good idea to object to a form of discipline while it is in progress (assuming that it doesn't physically harm your child). By waiting to discuss the incident with the adult in private and agreeing on a proper response for the future, you can avoid confusing your child even more. It is critical to stand up for your beliefs regarding discipline when dealing with both informal caregivers and child-care centers. If you are not in agreement with the adults who care for your child, you may need to find new caregivers who can carry out your wishes. If you are not sure that caregivers are responding as they say they are, try dropping in for a visit right before lunchtime, when toddlers tend to be at their worst, and observe the adults' behavior for yourself. By doing so, you may reassure yourself as well as your child.

"My Parents Spanked Me, and *I* Turned Out Okay."

Q: I was single when I gave birth to my son, David, and married when he was six months old. My husband is a much stricter parent than I am, and he tends to punish David when I feel he doesn't really deserve it. My husband says that's the way he was raised. David is nearly two now, and I've gotten better at arranging things so that he doesn't get into mischief as much as he used to. But my husband occasionally spanks him or hits him on the arm when he thinks he's misbehaving on purpose. I don't like to argue about his parenting behavior in front of David, but I don't like to stand by while he hits my child. What should I do?

A: While it's not a good idea to argue about parenting techniques in front of your child, physical abuse of any kind constitutes an exception. By striking your child, your husband is violating a trust between the two of you and between himself and David. It's best to step in at that point, removing your child from the scene. Once you have separated your husband and child, allow your husband to cool down, and then discuss the incident with him. Ask him if he really believes that hitting is the only answer and if so, why. He may not know that other options work. If possible, provide him with solid evidence (in the form of magazine articles and books) backing up your conviction that physical punishment is a bad idea. Suggest that he talk about this with other parents. If he continues hitting your child, enroll in parenting classes with him or, if the situation warrants, seek counseling as soon as possible. You owe it to your child—and your relationship with your husband—to work out this critical issue as soon as possible, since it will exist throughout your parenting careers.

MOVING FROM DISCIPLINE TOWARD SELF-DISCIPLINE

Of course, we all wish that our children would just behave without having to be disciplined or watched every single minute. Only near the end of this year, though, will your child's cognitive, emotional, verbal, and motor skills come together in a way that enables her to understand and follow rules more consistently. Once she is able to understand, remember, and decide to follow specific rules, she will move gradually toward understanding the principles behind them (that is, she will understand that it's bad to hurt any living thing, not just that it's bad to pull the cat's tail). Her full ability to understand these principles may not develop until she has passed her second birthday, but you can pave the way toward self-discipline this year by creating a structure upon which she can build general concepts of appropriate versus inappropriate behaviors later on.

The kind of reasoning that leads to effective self-discipline is *inductive* reasoning, the kind of thinking spurred by remarks you make such as "When you yell at me, it hurts my feelings," and "Don't push him, or he'll fall and cry." Sharing this insight into the effects of certain behaviors helps children understand the principles behind their parents'—and, eventually, society's—rules. It also allows them to internalize those principles. Though inductive reasoning is a sophisticated form of thinking that does not become possible until around the second birthday at the earliest, you can help your child begin to think this way by stimulating her verbal development (through talking and reading to her), cognitive skills (by playing with her), motor development (through drawing and physical activity), and social/emotional skills (by encouraging interaction with other children, sharing tasks, and taking turns).

Until your child becomes capable of inductive reasoning, prevention is still the best policy. Installing a baby gate at the top of the stairs is more effective with a twelve-month-old than explaining that if she tries to climb down the stairs she may get hurt. As she becomes more aware of the concepts of sequence, and cause and effect, however, you can begin to introduce her to the idea that there are natural consequences to her actions ("If you run away from me one more time, we'll have to go home") and the concept of having to wait before she's allowed to do something

One-year-olds' mobility and natural curiosity are a dangerous combination. Prevention, such as childproofing unsafe areas, is still the best approach.

("Don't open your present yet"). As she becomes more verbally adept, she will grow more interested in cooperative and other prosocial behavior ("It's time to clean up now"). These concepts will gradually lead to an ability to consider the other reasons behind most of your behavioral rules.

By age three, your child will be generally capable of understanding why one kind of behavior is good and another is bad. Until then, you will have to work within her limitations, always explaining the reasons behind your rules as simply as possible but understanding that she will not comprehend them fully in this year. In the meantime, your efforts to communicate these reasons to her will let her know that you care about those reasons and that you expect her to adopt them herself someday. This evidence of your concern is worth a thousand unexplained do's and don'ts—and will pay off eventually in a self-disciplined, rather than an oft-disciplined, child.

IF YOU'RE CONCERNED
Is My Child Spoiled?

No matter who you are or where you come from, your beliefs and others' regarding proper child-rearing are probably very different. You may deny your toddler's request that you buy her a toy, too, when shopping for her friend's birthday present ("We're shopping for Mary now"), while your mother may casually toss a present for your daughter into the shopping basket. Since your mother is acting according to what she believes is a reasonable belief system, how is it possible to know if she is spoiling your child? Is it even possible to spoil a person at this age?

Yes, it is possible, but definitions vary. It is important to keep in mind that an occasional tantrum doesn't necessarily mean your child is spoiled—it just means she's a toddler. Emotional extremes are a hallmark of the one- and two-year-old's experience, and the occasional meltdown is only to be expected as your child learns to deal with her feelings. Spoiled children, on the other hand, exhibit more deliberate misbehavior, and chances are that when one looks back on these children's lives, one will see that the seeds for their misbehavior were planted early. Inconsistency on the part of the parents is what makes it possible for children to learn to manipulate adults. A child's process of testing the adult over and over to see if the adult will set limits on her behavior can reach the point at which no one (adults included) wants to be around the child. Her behavior can lead to future relationship difficulties, which certainly no one wants.

Experts agree that the spoiled child is expressing a real need for discipline through her behavior, and her caregivers' refusal to provide it leads to increased anxiety and "acting out" behavior. For this reason, deciding on clear limits for your child and sticking to them consistently is a great service to the both of you. The clearer the rules are, the more easily she can follow them. A child who knows your unequivocal position on candy at the checkout stand will probably not bother to tease you about it, but if you vacillate on the issue, sometimes buying candy and sometimes not, you can expect a tantrum if you don't buy it *this* time. If you find you cannot control your child's behavior on a regular basis, it is time to sit down and work out some ground rules, allowing for a reasonable amount of slack (casually looking the other way when your child *sniffs* the candy bars at the checkout stand)— and make a point of sticking to them in the future.

"GOOD GIRL!"

It's a year later, and once again the family is in a mad morning rush to get out the door. Emily, now twenty-four months, strides into the bathroom, climbs up on her stool, and plucks her toothbrush from its holder. While looking for her toothpaste, her eyes happen to fall on the open toilet—an especially tempting receptacle since she's started the toilet-training process recently. She leans toward the toilet, lifts her toothbrush to drop it in, and hears her father's voice ring forth: "Emily! What are you doing?"

The sharp tone of her father's voice stops Emily's arm midthrow. In that moment's hesitation, she remembers the last time she tried to throw something into the toilet—and the time before. Straightening up, Emily turns to look at her dad with wide eyes.

Fred knows from experience that this is time to change the subject. "Were you about to brush your own teeth, all by yourself?" he says. "What a big girl!" Emily's face relaxes as she turns back to the mirror. In the reflection, she sees a big girl who can brush her own teeth.

"I do it!" she says proudly. Then, holding her toothbrush high in the air to show her dad, she gets to work on the toothpaste tube.

Fred gives his daughter a pat on the head and starts off to look for his shoes again. But then, on second thought, he returns to the bathroom—and removes the open tube of toothpaste before Emily has a chance to "brush" the entire mirror.

A D V A N C E S

Advances Toward Self-Discipline in the Second Year

12 MONTHS	Begins imitating some adult actions
	Enjoys demonstrating mastery
	Understands that she can cause things to happen
18 MONTHS	May follow simple commands
	May be aware of cause and effect
	Memory starts to improve
	Begins to understand concepts behind simple safety issues (hot stove, etc.)
24 MONTHS	Begins to understand simple time-related concepts ("soon," "after breakfast," etc.)
	Starts to rely more on words to communicate feelings

FIRST-PERSON SINGULAR

No matter how "naughty or nice" your child has been this year, it's sure to have been (literally!) a challenging period. Take a few minutes to record here the triumphs that you most want to remember—the first time your child pulled a chair over to watch while you made dinner or the first time she put away her toys without even being asked. Make a note of the kinds of limit-setting techniques that worked best with her—offering her a choice of acceptable behaviors and letting her pick one or discussing the reasons behind your decision until she felt she understood them. Chances are the techniques that work best now may also work well when she's a teenager. You may be glad later that you took some notes!

READER'S NOTES

_____

_____

_____

_____

_____

_____

_____

_____

_____

_____

CHAPTER 9

Looking Ahead—I'm Two

H e can walk, he can talk, and now the real fun is about to begin.

It's been a long year but a very fruitful one for the children we've observed in these chapters. In twelve months, Philip and Tara, Spencer and Clara— and your own one-year-old—have learned to walk, feed themselves, communicate verbally, and deepen their relationships with loved ones as well as with new friends. We have watched clear personalities emerge from their baby selves as they have learned to make their wishes known and their opinions heard. Though your own development as parents might not have seemed quite as mind-boggling on the surface, you know that your skills in effectively raising your child have improved as your knowledge about him has deepened. This knowledge will come in handy as your one-year-old turns two and faces the equally challenging transformations that occur in that year. You may be dreading the two-year-olds' legendary tantrums, refusals to eat, and insistence on doing everything themselves— but don't worry. With the empathy, communication skills, and humor you've developed over these past months, you'll be able to see these new developments as the exciting signs of growth and challenges to your creativity as a parent that they really are.

A LARGER WORLD:
WHAT YOUR CHILD HAS LEARNED

Motor development took center stage in your child's life this year, certainly during the first six months. This is the year in which he began walking with ease, climbing, and even running. His developmental process did not take place smoothly, but in fits and starts and perhaps even with a few regressions (or "touchpoints," as my colleague Dr. Brazelton would say). At its most intense, it might have disrupted your little one's sleep, prevented him from sitting still to eat or to be changed, and led to outbursts of frustration when you buckled him into a car seat or stroller. By his second birthday, though, he has clearly mastered his ability to get around, as well as to perform such fine-motor skills as feeding himself with a spoon and grasping a crayon. Though further refinement of his motor skills will certainly follow in the years to come, they will probably never again dominate his life to such a great extent.

Your one-year-old's great strides in movement skills were strongly linked to his increasingly urgent quest for independence. During this year, he began to test the ground between independence and attachment, as each need triggered its opposite drive. This balancing act between the urge to explore and the need for Mom and Dad will continue into his third year. You are quite likely to continue to hear the proud announcement "I did it myself!" as well as soft bedtime requests for a story and cuddle—and cries of frustration ("I can't do it!") when the balance between not enough parental presence or too much of it feels wrong.

Throughout this year, your child's physical development—and the independent exploration that took place as a result—has stimulated a great deal of cognitive growth. By reaching, grasping, emptying, pushing, banging, filling, and otherwise experimenting with physical objects, your one-year-old learned a great deal about the physical nature of the world around him, including the concepts of space, cause and effect, and sequence. His practice with finding hidden or discarded objects (and his experience with your comings and goings) has led to a new understanding of what happens to things and people when they disappear from his sight. His memory improved tremendously, allowing him to learn more effectively from experience, to make a plan and carry it out, and to begin to learn rules of behavior. His ability to think symbolically led to new skills in imaginary play. At age eighteen months, he might have been able to pretend to drink from an empty cup; by his second birthday, he can imagine that something else (his teddy bear, perhaps) is drinking from that cup, and his imaginary play thus becomes richer and more satisfying.

Of course, all of these cognitive advances have fed into your one-year-old's stunning advances in the ability to use and understand language. He has grown from a babbling baby to a relatively sophisticated individual who expresses his opinions in two- three-, and maybe even four-word sentences. Master of perhaps one or two words at twelve months, he now knows as many as two hundred—and is picking up half a dozen or more each day. Instead of crying to try to convey to you that something is wrong (but *what?*) he can now tell you exactly how he feels. Chances are he can also use his verbal skills to reach out to new friends and frame his thoughts and experiences in conscious memories that will stay with him in the years to come.

All of this development—physical, mental, emotional, and verbal— has set the stage for the magical blossoming of his personality. As his likes and dislikes, needs and wants, and fears and enthusiasms have been made manifest, he has begun to turn noticeably outward to engage with the outside world. His realization at around twelve months that he and others possess a private mental and emotional world led to a growing awareness of (and fascination with) the concepts of the "self" versus "another." His developing verbal abilities increasingly allowed him to express his own inner thoughts and explore those of others. He became aware of his loved ones' separate emotional states and began to respond to their emotions as well as to events that affected him directly. He learned to empathize to some degree with the other children in his life and grew fascinated by their own ways of coping with the world. Gradually, his interest in others' subjective viewpoints led him to sense a pattern of "principles" or beliefs behind your creation of a daily routine and your setting of limits. Increasingly, he moved from mainly wanting to please himself (by satisfying his urge to explore) toward wanting to please you and his other caregivers by being "good" and following your rules.

TRUSTING YOURSELF:
WHAT YOU HAVE LEARNED

The year has been one of great discoveries for you as well as for your child. The months between ages one and two brought with them the miracle of your child's "unveiling." By now, whether you worked at home or away from the house this year, you know your child as no one else does. You know his temperament—whether he is generally calm and easygoing or sensitive and easily upset, active and assertive or shy and secretive, reckless and adventurous or cautious and slow. You also know where his temperament and yours match and where they clash, and you've begun to experiment with ways to accommodate these differences.

Your second year of closely observing your little one's physical and emotional growth has given you a greater understanding of his capabilities and needs. As a result, you can more effectively tailor your expectations and his tasks to suit him. You can avoid pressuring him to master a skill (toilet training, for example) before he's ready and can more easily trust yourself to recognize any developmental or health problems that arise.

After a year of increasingly sophisticated conversation, you have to guess much less about your child's wants, needs, passions, and opinions. By now you usually know what he's saying, even if your friends and relatives don't. The two of you have learned how to communicate effectively; he is better able to understand your speech, and you are continuing to help him develop his. This new level of communication is more than just a skill. Through words, your child can open his mind to you, giving you a much better idea of where he is in his development and emotional growth. This greater knowledge allows you to continue to stay one step ahead of him, leading him toward greater understanding and more complex thought and action.

WHAT'S NEXT?: DEVELOPMENT
IN THE THIRD YEAR

The seeds planted in the second year truly blossom in the third, making age two an especially satisfying time for both parent and child. Your child will experience another great burst of development as his third year begins. The continued refinement of his fine-motor skills will make him more adept at such tasks as dressing himself, drawing, turning the pages of a book, and playing with more complex toys. His increased ability will lower his frustration level (and your own) as he works at these tasks, but his need to "do it himself" means you will have to plan for the extra time (and patience) it takes to get those things done.

After age twenty-four months, toilet training may be begun with greater chance of success. Your child is likely to take quite a bit of pride now in tending to his own bodily functions and become curious about wearing "big kid" underwear or using the bathroom like his older siblings or friends. Though he will be prone to a number of "accidents" this year, your patience and support will help him gradually master this skill. Due to physical limitations, however, he may continue to need pull-ups at night as late as his fourth or fifth year.

Your child's developing social awareness in the third year will help you continue to promote such prosocial behavior as sharing, taking turns, and speaking politely. His desire to live up to your standards (along with his urge to test them) will continue to increase as the one-year-old's irresistible urge to touch everything subsides. Your continued, consistent setting of limits will help him develop self-discipline, and his greater experience with inductive reasoning (pulling Suzie's hair makes her cry; if I run on the wall, I may fall off) will allow him to understand why he can't do certain things. Finally his expanding sense of time will enable you to say "in a minute" or "later" and have a reasonable hope that he will understand and briefly accept the concept.

The third year is a wonderful time for making friends and learning new social skills. As a two-year-old, your child will learn a great deal by imitating others, especially same-age or slightly older children. He will become interested in all the rituals and rules of friendship, from a habitual hug hello to the house rule that cookies be shared. His expanding imagination will allow him to enjoy playing with (rather than alongside) his peers more, and his ability to empathize, laugh at others' jokes, and "be funny" himself will help him cement his bonds with them.

Perhaps the most exciting area of growth in the third year is in language development. Your child's communication skills will advance at a

Between ages two and three, peer relationships blossom as children enjoy sharing their discoveries with new friends.

rocket pace next year. For the first time, he will be able to make use of the basic rules of grammar, and his more sophisticated language skills allow for increasingly complex symbolic thinking. When he becomes a two-year-old, your child's questions will increase in number, and they won't stop coming. Your life will be filled with "Wazzat?" and "Where it goed?" Your child is likely to repeat the same questions over and over, partly to ensure that your answer is always the same and perhaps also to reexperience the pleasure of a successful communication.

If language growth is one of the greatest satisfactions in the third year, emotional swings may turn out to be the greatest challenge. For at least the first half of the third year, your child's negativism may be at its most extreme, caused in large part by his steadily increasing determination to control and manage his world. Spurts of cognitive growth (language and abstract concepts) or physical development (toilet training) may again disrupt his sleep for brief periods, as his mind races so fast or his body can't slow down after a particularly exciting and challenging day. Fortunately, you know your child much better now. Your deeper understanding of his temperament, moods, needs, and desires will go far in helping you weather the inevitable storms of early childhood—and in allowing you, your child, and your family to enjoy the many good days ahead.

FIRST-PERSON SINGULAR

Now is a wonderful time to turn back to the beginning of this book and read the predictions you wrote down twelve months ago about what you thought your child might be like at age two. How accurate were your guesses? In what ways did your child surprise you? This might also be a good time to get out any videotapes and photographs you have and take a look at all the ways he's advanced over the year. Once you've properly appreciated his progress, write down some predictions here about the year to come. What are your goals for your child, for yourself as a parent, and for your family as a whole this year? In what ways would you most like to see your child grow? Have you noticed any particularly strong skills yet, or do you suspect that one or more might develop next year? As we've seen, the better you know your one-of-a-kind child, the better equipped you will be to help him grow. Thinking about him with pen in hand provides you both with tools for a better future as well as memories to look back on in the years to come.

READER'S NOTES

_____

_____

_____

_____

_____

_____

_____

_____

_____

_____

_____

_____

_____

_____

_____

_____

_____

_____

BIBLIOGRAPHY

Begley, Sharon. "Your Child's Brain." *Newsweek,* Feb. 19, 1996.

Brazelton, T. Berry. *Touchpoints: Your Child's Emotional and Behavioral Development.* Reading, Mass.: Perseus Books, 1992.

Cole, Michael, and Cole, Sheila R. *The Development of Children,* 3rd edition. New York: W. H. Freeman and Company, 1996.

Dunn, Judy. *The Beginning of Social Understanding.* Cambridge, Mass.: Harvard University Press, 1988.

"Fertile Minds." *Time,* Feb. 13, 1997.

Gopnik, Alison M.; Meltzoff, Andrew N.; and Kuhl, Patrica K. *The Scientist in the Crib: Minds, Brains, and How Children Learn.* New York: William Morrow and Co., 1999.

Kopp, Claire B. *Baby Steps: The "Whys" of Your Child's Behavior in the First Two Years.* New York: W. H. Freeman and Company, 1994.

Lieberman, Alicia. *The Emotional Life of the Toddler.* New York: Free Press, 1993.

Markman, Ellen M. *Categorization and Naming in Children: Problems of Induction* (MIT Series in Learning, Development, and Conceptual Change). Cambridge, Mass.: Bradford Books, 1991.

Newcombe, Nora. *Child Development: Change Over Time.* New York: HarperCollins, 1996.

"Read*Write*Now*." www.ed.gov

Shore, Rima. *Rethinking the Brain: New Insights into Early Development.* New York: Families and Work Institute, 1997.

Sroufe, Alan; Cooper, Robert G.; Dehart, Ganie B.; and Marshall, Mary E. *Child Development: Its Nature and Course,* 3rd edition. New York: McGraw-Hill, 1996.

Stern, Daniel N. *Diary of a Baby: What Your Child Sees, Feels, and Experiences.* New York: Basic Books. 1998.

"Your Child: From Birth to Three." *Newsweek Special Edition.* Spring/Summer, 1997.

RECOMMENDED READINGS

CHAPTER 1 **What I'm Like**
Brazelton, T. Berry. *Toddlers and Parents* (revised ed.). New York: Delacorte Press/Lawrence, 1989.

———. *Touchpoints: Your Child's Emotional and Behavioral Development.* Reading, Mass.: Perseus Books, 1992.

Kopp, Claire B. *Baby Steps: The "Whys" of Your Child's Behavior in the First Two Years.* New York: W. H. Freeman and Company, 1994.

Shelov, Steven, and Robert E. Hanneman (eds.), American Academy of Pediatrics. *Caring for Your Baby and Young Child: Birth to Age 5.* New York: Bantam Doubleday Dell, 1998.

CHAPTER 2 **Starting the Motor—My Physical Abilities**
Spock, Benjamin, Steven Parker, and Stephen J. Parker. *Dr. Spock's Baby and Child Care* (7th ed.). New York: Pocket Books, 1998.

CHAPTER 3 **Thinking for Myself—My Cognitive Development**
Gardner, Howard. *Frames of Mind: The Theory of Multiple Intelligences* (10th anniversary ed.). New York: Basic Books, 1993.

Greenspan, Stanley and Serena Weider with Robin Simon. *The Child with Special Needs: Encouraging Intellectual and Emotional Growth.* Reading, Mass.: Perseus Books, 1998.

Stern, Daniel N. *Diary of a Baby: What Your Child Sees, Feels, and Experiences.* New York: Basic Books, 1998.

CHAPTER 4 **Listen to Me!—My Verbal Abilities**
Gopnik, Alison M., Andrew N. Meltzoff, and Patricia K. Kuhl. *The Scientist in the Crib: Minds, Brains and How Children Learn.* New York: William Morrow and Co., 1999.

Pinker, Steven. *The Language Instinct: How the Mind Creates Language.* New York: Harper-Perennial, 1995.

CHAPTER 5 **Tears and Laughter—My Emotional Growth**
Chess, Stella, and Alexander Thomas. *Know Your Child.* New York: Basic Books, 1987.

Greenspan, Stanley, and Nancy Thorndike Greenspan. *First Feelings.* New York: Viking, 1985.

Kagan, J. *The Nature of the Child.* New York: Basic Books, 1984.

Lieberman, Alicia, Ph.D. *The Emotional Life of the Toddler.* New York: Free Press, 1993.

Pruett, Kyle. *Fatherneed: Why Father Care Is as Essential as Mother Care for Your Child.* New York: Free Press, 2000.

CHAPTER 6 **Where I Stand—My Social Development**
Dunn, Judy. *The Beginnings of Social Understanding.* Cambridge, Mass.: Harvard University Press, 1988.

Greenspan, Stanley, with J. Salmon. *The Challenging Child: Understanding, Raising, and Enjoying the Five "Difficult" Types of Children.* Reading, Mass.: Addison-Wesley, 1997.

Hopson, Darlene Powell, and Derek S. Hopson. *Different and Wonderful: Raising Black Children in a Race-Conscious Society.* New York: Fireside, 1992.

Kagan, J., and S. Lamb (eds.). *The Emergence of Morality in Young Children.* Chicago: University of Chicago Press, 1988.

CHAPTER 8 **Drawing the Line—My Need for Limits**
Windell, James. *Discipline: A Sourcebook of 50 Failsafe Techniques for Parents.* New York: Macmillan, 1991.

ORGANIZATIONS AND
SUPPORT GROUPS

ADVICE AND RESOURCES FOR PARENTS
Family Resource Coalition
(312) 338-0900
Chicago, IL
This service puts callers in touch with state and local branches for accessible community support.

Gerber Information Line
(800) 443-7237
A twenty-four-hour information source, staffed by parents and grandparents. Offers advice on diapering, sleeping, feeding, and other nonmedical parenting issues.

National Parent Information Network
(800) 583-4135
Largest parenting database in the United States. Parents can call for free professional referrals, advice, and printed articles. Weekdays, 8:00 A.M.–5:00 P.M. CST.

Zero to Three
734 15th Street NW, Suite 1000
Washington, D.C. 20005
(202) 638-1144
www.zerotothree.org
Call this child-advocacy group for a general-information kit, or access its website for excellent information on all aspects of infant and toddler development.

On-line Resources
American Academy of Pediatrics
www.aap.org
The academy provides a wealth of information on the most recent scientific findings on teething, nightmares, toilet training, and countless other issues affecting children and their families.

Babycenter.com

www.babycenter.com

This website provides frequent updates on your child's development, as well as answers to parents' questions and a large database of information for parents.

Family.com

www.family.com

Sponsored by Disney, this website provides forums for parents to meet and talk online.

ParenthoodWeb

www.parenthoodweb.com

Answers to frequently asked questions. Pediatricians and psychiatrists also respond to parents' questions sent by e-mail.

Parenting Q&A

www.parenting-qa.com

Offers answers to parents' questions, reading lists and activity suggestions for kids, and other family services.

ParentSoup

www.parentsoup.com

A good source of on-line advice for parents for nearly every challenging situation.

ParenTalk Newsletter

www.tnpc.com/parentalk/index.html

An on-line collection of articles by psychologists and physicians for parents.

Totalbabycare.com

www.totalbabycare.com

Advice for parents on child development and parenting issues, sponsored by the Pampers Parenting Institute.

U.S. Department of Education

www.ed.gov

Provides ideas and resources for parents relating to early childhood education, including the excellent "Read*Write*Now*" Early Childhood Kit.

Child Care Aware
NACCRRA
1319 F Street NW, Suite 810
Washington, D.C. 20004
(800) 424-2246
www.naccrra.net
CCA provides referrals to local licensed and accredited child-care centers anywhere in the United States. They also offer a free information packet on how to choose quality child care. Weekdays, 9:00 A.M.–4:30 P.M. EST.

Families and Work Institute
330 Seventh Avenue
New York, NY 10001
(212) 465-2044
www.familiesandwork.org
Publishers of an excellent book for parents and professionals, *Rethinking the Brain: New Insights into Early Development* by Rima Shore, this organization provides information relating to the changing nature of work and family life.

SPECIAL NEEDS
Mothers United for Mutual Support
150 Custer Court
Green Bay, WI 54301
(414) 336-5333
Support and networking for families of children with any disorder, delay, or disability.

The National Organization of Mothers of Twins Club
P.O. Box 23188
Albuquerque, NM 87192-1188
(505) 275-0955
Offers advice and information to parents of twins or higher multiples and refers callers to local chapters.

CRISIS INTERVENTION
ChildHelp National Hotline
(800) 4-A-CHILD
Twenty-four-hour advice and referrals for children and adults with questions or in crisis. Staffers with graduate degrees in counseling answer the phone.

National Clearinghouse for Family Support/Children's Mental Health
(800) 628-1696
Twenty-four-hour information and referrals to local family clinics, support groups, and therapists.

SUPPORT GROUPS
National Association of Mothers' Centers
336 Fulton Avenue
Hempstead, NY 11550
(800) 645-3828
Provides referrals to mothers' support groups and centers in your area, as well as information on how to start a group.

Parents Anonymous
Claremont, CA
(909) 621-6184
(800) 932-HOPE
Provides referrals to state and local affiliates, which offer support groups, counseling, and referrals. Weekdays, 8:00 A.M.–4:30 P.M. PST.

Parents Without Partners
401 North Michigan Avenue
Chicago, IL 60611
(312) 644-6610
National organization with local chapters providing support for single parents.

INDEX

Page numbers in *italics* refer to illustrations.

fine- and gross-motor achievements of, 43, 202

overview of progress made by, 10–15, 202–3

major achievements made by, 22

parental support needed by, 8–9

relationships between, 88–89; *see also* social development

social achievements of, 132–34, 148–49

verbal achievements of, 80–82, 95–96, 203

organizations and support groups, 213–16

overstimulation, 57

parent-child combinations, uniqueness of, 2, 111

parenting:

from both parents, 119–22, *120*

flexibility in, 2

modeling good behavior and, 185–86

as process, 3

styles of, 138

Parent's Story sections, 17–18, 29–30, 50–51, 89, 101–2, 146–47, 154–55, 183–84

Parke, Ross, 119

peekaboo, 17, 18, 19, 36, 51, *62, 63*

peer pressure, 121

PET (positron emission tomography) scans, 48

physical abilities, 25–45

experimentation and, 40–42

fine-motor development, 34–38

motor achievements, 28–30

safety concerns, 38–40

walking, 25–27, 30–34

Pinker, Steven, 85

planning ahead, to avoid frustrations, 14–15, 118–19

play:

developmental importance of, 18–21, 61–65, *62,* 193

imaginative, 52

pacing of, 65–67

play dates, 12, 64, 133–34, 137–38, 147–48, 188

pointing gestures, *83*

positive reinforcement, 67, 119

positron emission tomography (PET) scans, 48

Power, T., 8

predictability, 60, 66, 151

see also routines

problem-solving difficulties, abuse and, 50

prosocial behavior, 139, 195, 205

Pruett, Kyle, 119

punishment, 186–90

Q&A sections, 3

on change of caregivers, 124

on child-care centers, 53

on climbing out of cribs, 156–57

on imitation, 56–57

on rejection of father, 121–22

on social development, 130–31

on spanking, 192

on swear words, 87

on verbal development, 93–94

Ramey, Craig, 16

reading aloud, 17, 67–69, *68,* 79, 193

"Read*Write*Now*," 78

receptive speech, 80

rechanneling, 145

recommended readings, 211–12

referencing, social, 132

regressions, 202

relationships, 50, 147–48

relaxing rituals, 160

repetition, 40

developmental importance of, 32

restaurants, eating in, 163–65

rewards, 185

rhythms, 31

of conversation, 88–89